⫸ W9-BNE-482

AN APPRECIATION

OF EASTERN

CHRISTIANITY

Rev. Clement C. Englert, C.SS.R.

RELIGION CENTER
ST. MARY, KENOSHA

LIGUORI PUBLICATIONS
Liguori, Missouri 63057

EcC
659
E

First published under the title: *Catholics and Orthodox — Can They Unite?* © 1961, New York. The present volume is a revised and updated edition of the original.

Imprimi Potest:
Joseph L. Kerins, C.SS.R.
Provincial, Philadelphia Province
Redemptorist Fathers
October 4, 1971

Imprimatur:
Philadelphia, December 27, 1971
+ A. Senyshyn
Metropolitan of Philadelphia
Ukrainian Catholic Archdiocese

Library of Congress Card Number: 78-189073

First Printing / March 1972
by Liguori Publications

Printed in U.S.A.

**DEDICATED
TO
OUR MOTHER OF
PERPETUAL HELP**

ABBREVIATIONS

The meaning of most of the abbreviations in this book is clear from the text. However, the following deserve further explanation.

PG *Patrologiae Cursus Completus, Series Graeca,* (Greek Fathers), ed. J.P. Migne, Paris 1857.

PL *Patrologiae Cursus Completus, Series Latina,* (Latin Fathers), ed. J.P. Migne, Paris 1844.

MG Latin text only of 81 Greek Fathers ed. J. P. Migne, Paris 1856.

TABLE OF CONTENTS

FOREWORD

Most of the theological chapters in this book appeared originally as a series of articles in the *Ark* magazine. They were written at the request of Archbishop Ambrose Senyshyn and under his inspiration.

Then they appeared in book form as one volume of the first Fides Series of the Paulist Press with the title *Catholics and Orthodox — Can They Unite?*

Since then the Second Vatican Council took place. One of the Council's enduring emphases was ecumenism. In what field of ecumenical endeavor should there be a stronger sense of urgency than in the relationship between Catholics and Orthodox — the two great bodies of Christians whose traditions go back to the apostles?

Yielding to the request of friends, I have decided to rewrite my previous articles, and having received full publication rights from the Paulist Press, to put out a new volume which will simply outline the questions discussed between Catholics and Orthodox. The bibliography can lead readers into deeper study of individual problems.

The differences between Catholics and Orthodox are not unbridgeably great. We share the same sources of faith — the Bible and Tradition. We venerate the same holy Church Fathers. We make use of the same seven sacraments. Our Church polity is built on the same divine orders of bishop, priest and deacon. The center of worship in East and West is the sacred Eucharistic liturgy.

What then keeps us apart? Aside from historic reasons — all enmeshed in politics, personalities, prejudices and nationalism — there is the matter of papal jurisdiction. There are, besides, some other smaller matters of belief and practice that would have to be studied together. What these problems are and how they might be solved form the subject matter of this book. At first glance these problems may seem too numerous and too insoluble to warrant high hopes for reunion. But people of good will on both sides could bring all to success.

Father George Tavard, A.A., long a student of separated Christianity, has remarked: "The Orthodox already believe in the infallibility of the Church. It is not too big a step from this to the infallibility of the Pope." Father Alexander Schmemann of St. Vladimir's Orthodox Seminary in New York has sagely remarked: "We can hardly expect that the Catholics will admit they have been wrong. But we might be able to show them that they did not always use the right words to phrase their beliefs."

The late lamented Pope John, who convoked the Second Vatican Council, and hoped that it would promote Christian unity, remarked that though the dogmas of faith cannot be changed, the formulations of them enjoy no such infallibility.

In the Second Vatican Council's decree on Ecumenism (Ch. 2, No. 11), we read the remarkable passage:

"When comparing doctrines with one another, they (theologians) should remember that in Catholic doctrine there exists an order or 'hierarchy' of truths, since these vary in their relation to the foundation of the Christian faith."

This thought was put forward at the Council by Archbishop Andrea Pangrazio of Gorizia (Italy) and supported by Cardinal Koenig of Vienna. Doctrines having to do with the Incarnation and Redemption, God's love and mercy to man, eternal life in God's kingdom are considered the foundation-doctrines of Christianity. Other matters like the number of the sacraments, worship, and the Church's hierarchical structure are considered to be on a lower level as means of salvation. (Cfr. Bernard Leeming, The Vatican Council and Christian Unity, New York, 1966, pp. 298-299).

The late great Archbishop of Lviv, Metropolitan Andrew Sheptitsky, whose cause of canonization has already been started, wrote a few years ago that most of the discrepancies between East and West were merely a matter of starting out from different angles to view different facets of the same truth, and that it was more a matter of two mentalities rather than two theologies that separated East and West.

Pope John gave the world two directives as a preparation for Church-reunion. One is positive: prayer for the Council's success. One is negative: forget the mistakes of the past, because there have been errors on both sides; look only to God's will for us in the future.

When all is said and done, no amount of mere theological discussion will ever succeed in uniting the Catholic and Orthodox Churches. What will do it? The grace of God. How is that obtained? By prayer. Whose prayers? The prayers of Christians of good will on both sides, and particularly the prayers of the holy Mother of God, who is loved and reverenced and glorified by the Orthodox as well as the Catholic Christians.

Surely our Lady cannot but bless the Christians of the East who call upon her with such ardor in every single service, in every part of the Divine Office, repeatedly in the Holy Liturgy — in fact, in almost every prayer in the ritual, where at least the phrase "by the prayers of the Mother of God" is inserted with the words of petition. She who is hymned daily as "more honorable than the Cherubim and incomparably more glorious than the Seraphim"; she who is hailed constantly as "the most holy, most immaculate, most blessed and glorious Lady, ever-virgin Mary and Mother of God"; she whose most popular picture in the Western Church, Our Lady of Perpetual Help, is a cultural product of the Eastern Church — she it is, the Madonna of the famed Byzantine icon, who will reunite all her children and lead them by the hand to her Son.

But if reunion depends so largely on prayer, why publish this book detailing our differences?

Because God, to accomplish His beneficent purposes, makes use of secondary causes (here, human beings). Students and theologians have to consider the matters that stand between us. Nothing but complete honesty will here serve a good purpose. In line with this thinking, Archbishop Humberto Madeiros of Boston, who formerly as Bishop of Brownsville, Texas was active in ecumenism there, remarked to his non-Catholic friends, that he would always respect their honesty by talking plainly about our differences of belief, yet always respecting their independence of conscience. And the distinguished Orthodox author and theologian, Father John Meyendorff, in a speech accepting the St. John Chrysostom award (Washington, D.C., 1968), remarked:

"Why not start a theological fellowship where the issues dividing or uniting us will be *studied* patiently, without haste or hope for immediate result . . . It may be that, in a task which required time and patience, others will by-pass us, but I am convinced that ultimately we will be accomplishing more useful work than many 'solemn assemblies.' "

Clement C. Englert, C.SS.R.

CHAPTER 1

THE EASTERN RITES OF CHRISTIANITY

Mass in the Early Church

How our Lord celebrated the first Mass is delineated in the New Testament accounts of the Last Supper. We have there portrayed for us the simplest elements of the Holy Sacrifice.

Our Lord took the bread and wine and prayed over them, offering them up to the Father with a blessing; then He consecrated them into His precious body and blood and gave them to the apostles in Holy Communion.

The Savior told the apostles to do the same thing in commemoration of Him. They did so faithfully. Wherever they preached the Gospel, they also celebrated the Eucharist. At first the Jewish-Christian converts continued to frequent the Temple in Jerusalem and go to the synagogues, reserving the celebration of the Eucharist until the evening, when it was usually joined to the meal they then took. In this way they imitated our Lord when He instituted the Blessed Sacrament at an evening meal.

But soon the persecution of Christians by the Jewish authorities set in. Eventually the Temple of Jerusalem was destroyed. More and more thousands of Gentiles were entering the Church. It became quite impossible to frequent the synagogue and be a Christian, too.

However, the Christian Church did borrow something from the synagogue which it never gave up: the service we call the *Mass of the Catechumens.* Today it is called the Liturgy of the Word. For some time the Christians held their own synagogue or *Mass of the Catechumens* service in the morning and celebrated the Eucharist in the evening in conjunction with a meal or supper called the Agape ("love feast").

But it became increasingly difficult for people to gather twice for service on Sundays. Moreover, the great era of persecutions (64-313 A.D.) made it necessary to assemble secretly. Thus, at an early date, it became customary to join the synagogue service and the celebration of the Eucharist into one sacred function. That gave us the Mass in its present broad outline.

First there was the *Mass of the Catechumens* — so called because the catechumens (i.e. converts taking instructions to join the Church) were allowed to be present only at the first part or synagogue-service. It is called today the Liturgy of the Word because readings from Sacred Scripture, the Word of God, are its chief feature. Then followed the *Mass of the Faithful,* so called because only the baptized believers could be present when the Eucharist was celebrated. Today this is called the Liturgy of the Eucharist (literally "thanksgiving") because the Mass proper or confection of the holy sacrament of the Eucharist takes place now — the characteristic-Christian service.

Although both Saturday and Sunday were kept

holydays in the early years of Christianity, the Sunday soon became the preferred day because our Lord rose from the dead on a Sunday, and the Holy Spirit came down upon the Apostles on the first Pentecost on a Sunday.

As a remnant of the early state of things, however, Saturday remains a liturgical day in the East, though Sunday is the day of obligation. In the Byzantine rite, for example, the Saturdays of Lent are not fast days (except Holy Saturday) and the liturgy is always celebrated on Saturday. Many Saturdays of the year have proper liturgies like the Sundays.

The persecutions lasted more than 200 years, until the Emperor Constantine issued the decree of toleration in 313, known as the Edict of Milan. It granted freedom in the exercise of their religion to Christians and all other religious sects. Christians could then come out of hiding, begin to build churches and basilicas, and hold services freely — as often and as long as they wished.

For the first 300 or 400 years of Christianity, the Mass was in a fluid state — there were no fixed rules on how it must be celebrated. Everywhere, of course, the same general pattern was observed. There were chants (hymns and psalms), readings from Sacred Scripture (from the Old Testament and from whatever manuscripts they could obtain of the New Testament), public prayer led by the clergy and a sermon by the bishop or priest celebrating the service.

Then the bread and wine were brought to the altar (often offered by the people themselves, along with gifts for the clergy); the presiding bishop or priest blessed these gifts and offered to God what was to be used for the Eucharist. Then he recited aloud a prayer of thanksgiving (the Preface), in which he thanked God for all His benefits, for creation, for redemption, for this Holy Sacrifice given us by our Lord himself on the night before He died.

If the bishop or priest celebrating was particularly emotional or oratorical, the Preface might turn out to be a long prayer. If the celebrant was a simple man, it was apt to be brief and direct. The Consecration followed, with some prayers of adoration and petition. The Lord's Prayer introduced the Communion. The presiding clergyman led in prayers of thanksgiving, a blessing was given, and the Mass was over.

This simple outline of the liturgy in the early Church already appears in the writings of St. Justin the Martyr, who flourished in the middle of the second century.

Origin of Rites

As churches were built in the fourth century, definite patterns of worship began to appear and the great Churches in the cities developed their own characteristic liturgies. The number of lessons from Scripture, the place of the hymns, the processions of clergy and people, the use of incense, the definite pattern of vestments — all these things gradually became fixed. Hence, there grew up the chief liturgical families or rites: at Rome, at Alexandria (in Egypt), at Antioch (in Syria) and eventually at Constantinople (the Eastern capital of the Greco-Roman Empire).

From these great centers of population and Christianity, the missionaries spread out to convert the neighboring country. Naturally they carried with them the form of liturgy used in the Mother Church. Where the mission was distant, variations crept in, so that eventually almost a new rite was formed. Thus the Eastern Syrians in Iraq and Persia came to differ from the Syrians at Antioch; and the

Abyssinians (or Ethiopians), who received their faith from Alexandria in Egypt, developed their own form of the Coptic (Egyptian) rite.

The bishops of the chief centers of Christianity were called patriarchs, and the territories over which they ruled as presiding bishops were called patriarchates. This was definitely sanctioned by the early Church Councils held in 325 at Nicea and in 381 at Constantinople.

Arianism

When Arius, a priest of Alexandria, taught that the second Person of the Blessed Trinity was not equal to the Father, or true God, but merely a creature much more perfect than other creatures, the seeds of heresy were spread. Accordingly, the bishops of the Catholic world, gathered together at the Council of Nicea in Asia Minor in 325, declared him a heretic. Although some individuals lost their faith, no whole nation was cut off from the Church because of Arianism.

Nestorians and Chaldeans

When Nestorius of Constantinople taught that in Christ there are two Persons as well as two natures, and that our Lady is therefore only the Mother of the human person Christ, the bishops met at the Council of Ephesus in 431 and condemned this doctrine, and proclaimed Mary to be the Mother of God, the *Theotokos*.

Some Syrians refused to accept the decision and left the Church, fleeing to the Persian Empire. They carried on extensive missionary work, spreading their form of Christianity far to the East and down into India. The Nestorian Church still survives in the Near East, very reduced in numbers. There are a few in the United States.

Those who returned to the Catholic Church from

the Nestorians in Eastern Syria form what we call today the Chaldean rite. Their chief bishop, called the patriarch of Babylon, lives at Mosul in Iraq. There are about 195,000 of them. A few hundred are in the United States, and they have a small parish in Chicago and another in Detroit.

Many Christians in India also returned to the Catholic Church in the 16th century and form the Syro-Malabar rite, which has been somewhat latinized. Their chief prelate is the Archbishop of Ernakulam. They number well over a million souls and are in a flourishing condition. They are not represented in America.

The Monophysites

In opposing the Nestorians, some enthusiasts went too far in the other direction and taught that our Lord's human nature was swallowed up in the divine. Hence they were called Monophysites, literally the "one-nature-men." This heresy was condemned by the Catholic bishops at the Council of Chalcedon in 451. Again many refused to submit to the decision of the Council that in Christ there is one divine Person and two distinct natures, the human and the divine. Many Syrians left the Church and became known as Jacobites.

Those who returned to Catholic unity from among the Jacobites belong to the rite called the Pure Syrian rite. They number about 87,000. Their chief bishop is called the patriarch of Antioch and lives at Beirut, Lebanon. There are a few hundred in the United States, but they have no churches of their own and usually frequent the churches of the Maronite rite.

A group of Indian Christians using the Pure-Syrian rite in a native form returned to the Catholic Church with their great leader Mar Ivanios in 1930. They form the Malankara rite. They number over

200,000. Their chief prelate is the Archbishop of Trivandrum, India. They are not represented in America.

The Monophysites in Egypt also separated from the rest of the Church, taking the majority of the faithful of the Alexandrian or Coptic rite. Since the Ethiopians were dependent on Egypt, they followed the example of the Egyptians. Those who returned to Catholic unity from among the Egyptian Monophysites form the Catholic Coptic rite. Their chief bishop is the patriarch of Alexandria who lives at Cairo. They number about 80,000. They are not represented in America. The Ethiopian Catholics number about 50,000 with an Archbishop and one Bishop in Abyssinia, and one Bishop in Eritrea. They are not represented in America.

The Melkite Rite

Since most Syrians and Egyptians were now separated from the rest of the Church, the faithful who remained turned more and more to Constantinople (or Byzantium, as it was originally called) for the protection of the Emperor. They became known as Melkites, literally the "king's-men."

Eventually they lost their Syrian and Coptic rites and adopted that of Byzantium which they keep to the present day. They number about 300,000. Their chief bishop is called the patriarch of Antioch and lives at Damascus. There are about 55,000 in the United States in 27 parishes. Recently they opened a seminary for their rites at Methuen in the Boston archdiocese. They now form a diocese of their own with a bishop living near Boston.

The Armenian Rite

The Armenians, the first people to embrace Christianity as a nation, developed a rite of their own. The origins of this rite go back to Antiochene and Byzantine sources. The Armenians sided with the Monophysites and left the Church after the Council of Chalcedon in 451. Eventually many returned to Catholic unity. They now number about 100,000. Their chief bishop is called the patriarch of Cilicia. He lives at Beirut. The non-Catholic Armenians are often called Gregorian Armenians, after St. Gregory the Illuminator who brought Christianity to their country in the fourth century. They have a patriarch at Etchmiazin in Soviet Armenia. They are spread throughout the Near East and are also in the United States.

The Maronite Rite

The Maronites are a group of Syrians who retired into the mountains of Lebanon for better protection against political and religious enemies. When they met the crusaders in the 12th century, they immediately proclaimed their union with the Catholic Church. It is their proud boast that they were really never formally separated from it. They adopted some features of the Roman rite from the crusaders and are the only Eastern rite Church that has no non-Catholic counterpart.

They follow the Syrian rite and their chief bishop is called the patriarch of Antioch. He lives at Bekerkeh in Lebanon. The Maronites number about 533,000. They are well represented in America, numbering over 100,000 and having 46 parishes. The Maronites in the United States also form a diocese and have their own bishop.

The Byzantine Rite

The two greatest rites in the Church are the Roman rite and the Byzantine rite. All of Western Europe belonged to the Roman patriarchate and practiced some Latin rite more or less like that of Rome itself. Some ancient variants of the Western

Latin rite are still to be found in old monastic orders like the Dominicans, the Carmelites, the Cistercians and the Carthusians. They also exist in the cities of Milan in Italy, Lyons in France, Toledo in Spain, and Braga in Portugal. The Roman rite has been carried round the world by the missionaries from Roman rite countries.

The Byzantine rite was followed by those in the Constantinople patriarchate. Greek missionaries converted Eastern Europe and brought their rite with them. The great Sts. Cyril and Methodius converted many of the Slavs and translated the Greek liturgy into the Slavonic language. St. Cyril composed an alphabet for the Slavs, which is the parent of the modern Russian, Ukrainian, Serbian and Bulgarian letters — which are still called "Cyrillic." Although the Poles, Czechs, Slovenians and most Slovaks and Croatians belong to the Roman rite, other great Slav nations like the Russians, the Ukrainians, the Serbs, and the Bulgars, belong to the Byzantine rite. Most Rumanians, some Albanians and Hungarians, and some of the people of Southern Italy and Sicily, also belong to the Byzantine rite. The majority of those who practice the Byzantine rite (often called popularly "the Greek rite") are not Greeks, but Slavs, and these people still use the ancient Slavonic language in the liturgy. The Rumanians and Hungarians use their own vernacular (today's spoken) language in the liturgy. The Byzantines of Southern Italy and Greece still use Greek. The use of English in the liturgy is growing steadily among Byzantine Christians in the United States.

In the year 1054, the Patriarch of Constantinople precipitated a schism from the Catholic Church and eventually most of the East followed after him. The story of the schism is one of politics, mutual misunderstandings and personalities — a sad chapter in the Church's history.

The Byzantine Catholics of Southern Italy never were separated from the Church. Groups of Christians from all the other nations of Eastern Europe eventually came back into union with the Catholic Church. Hence, today we have the great bodies of Ukrainian, Podcarpathian, Rumanian and Hungarian Catholics of the Byzantine rite, with smaller groups of Greeks and Russians. Those not in union with the Catholic Church are called "Eastern Orthodox." Those in union with the pope are called "Eastern Catholics," or "Greek rite" Catholics. They should not be called "Uniates." This term was used as an epithet of opprobrium by the enemies of reunion. It resembles the term "Papists" used in England during the Reformation.

In the United States there is no Catholic-Greek parish or Italo-Greek parish. There are 17 parishes of Rumanians served by ten priests. They number about 10,000. There are small Russian parishes in Los Angeles, San Francisco, Chicago and New York.

All the Eastern-rite Catholics in the United States are under the Roman-rite Bishops' jurisdiction, except the Ukrainians and Ruthenians, as well as the Melchites and Maronites, as mentioned above. The Ukrainian Catholics have an archbishop in Philadelphia and dioceses named Stamford (Conn.) and St. Nicholas of Chicago. These three sees embrace the whole territory of the United States. In Canada the country is divided into four Catholic-Ukrainian dioceses with the archbishop in Winnipeg, Manitoba.

The Podcarpathians (Russians, Hungarians, Croatians), often called Ruthenians, have an archbishop at Hunhall, Pa. and two other dioceses with bishops in Passaic, N.J. and Parma, Ohio.

Ukrainian Catholics in the United States number some 285,000 in 184 parishes. The Ruthenians number 273,000 in 202 parishes. Slav-Byzantine Catholics in Canada number about 300,000.

The majority of the Russians and Greeks are Orthodox, that is, not in union with Rome. In the United States there are several millions of Orthodox Christians. Their dioceses are organized on national-origin lines: Russian, Greek, Syrian, Rumanian, Albanian, Ukrainian, etc.

CHAPTER 2

EÁSTERN WORSHIP

Obviously, a short, general review of this kind cannot give anything like a full picture of the Mass in each of the rites. Since the Byzantine rite is by far the most widespread among both Eastern Catholics and Eastern Orthodox, we shall confine ourselves to the description of some of the ritual features of the Byzantine rite. Many of these features may be found in other rites, and where they are not to be found, it may be that the Eastern rite in question follows the Roman usage.

The Sign of the Cross

A Byzantine Christian makes the sign of the cross in a manner slightly different from the Western form. The hand moves first to the right shoulder and then to the left. The tips of the thumb, index and middle fingers are held together as a sign of belief in the Holy Trinity — three Persons in one God — while the remaining two fingers are closed together against the palm of the hand as a sign of faith in the two natures, human and divine, that are united in the one divine Person of Jesus Christ.

As a gesture of piety this sign of the cross is made again and again during a Byzantine service. Usually it is made by the priest and the people whenever mention occurs of the Persons of the Holy Trinity. It is also made in conjunction with a bow — more or less profound, depending upon the piety and physique of the worshiper — instead of a genuflection.

The priest blesses the people with his hand six times during the liturgy. In giving a blessing the priest holds his fingers in a ritually prescribed position: with the five fingers of his right hand, he forms the letters IC-XC, which are the first and last letters of the sacred names — Jesus Christ — in the old Greek alphabet. The index finger points straight out to form I; the middle and little fingers curve to form C, twice; the thumb is crossed over the fourth finger to form X. This symbolism is a reminder that the priest acts in the name of Jesus Christ, and that all blessings flow from Him.

Vestments

The Byzantine vestments resemble the Roman in origin. The stole is long and joined together in the front; the cincture is a band of cloth matching the other vestments; the priest wears a cuff at each wrist; the chasuble resembles a Roman cope, with the front solid across the chest and the lower front cut away. Both the Roman and the Byzantine chasubles had the same origin: the original chasuble fell to the floor on all sides. In the West the sides were gradually cut off to facilitate the priest's movements; in the East the lower front was gradually cut off for the same purpose.

Liturgical Colors

In the Byzantine rite there is no strict sequence of colors. Traditionally the rule is stated: bright colors are to be used on feast days; dark colors are proper for days of fast or of mourning.

In ancient times this rule was carried out by using chiefly two colors: white and dark red, and these are still the most frequently used in Byzantine churches. However, light blue, yellow, gold and pink are often used for white. Dark blue, green, purple or violet are used for red.

The Maronites and the Malabarese have adopted the Roman vestments; the Armenians and Chaldeans use a chasuble which is quite like a Roman cope without the hood. The Armenians also wear a richly ornamented collar which stands up stiffly on the shoulders over the other vestments.

Incense

The Eastern Christians use incense more frequently than required in the Roman rite. Before each important part of the Mass the altar, sanctuary and people are incensed in preparation for the ceremony about to take place.

Liturgical Language

Various languages are used at Mass by Christians of Eastern rite. The Maronites and Chaldeans use Syriac for the Anaphora or Canon of their Mass. Syriac is almost the same language as Aramaic, which was spoken by our Lord while He lived on earth. It is related to the ancient Hebrew and is a dead language.

The pure Syrian, the Malabar and the Malankara rites also use Syriac.

The Melkites celebrate Mass chiefly in Arabic, the spoken language of most of the countries of the Near East. They use some Greek at will, and on occasion celebrate the whole Mass in the original Greek.

The Armenians use an old classical form of

Armenian. The Hungarians and Rumanians celebrate Mass in their own languages.

All the Slav peoples using the Byzantine Rite — the Russians, Ruthenians, Ukrainians, Serbs, Bulgars — celebrate the liturgy in the old Slavonic language, still employing the ancient alphabet invented for them by St. Cyril. This language is a dead language, and hence — like Latin and Greek and Syriac — is not subject to change.

The Maronites and Chaldeans have introduced the custom of using their vernacular Arabic instead of ancient Syriac for the Mass of the Catechumens or at least for the reading of the lessons and the Gospel. In many of the Byzantine churches in America, one hears the lessons or even the whole Mass read in English instead of Old Slavonic or the language of national origin.

Holy Communion

In the Byzantine rite, Holy Communion is given to the people under both species with a golden spoon. Leavened bread is used.

At Communion time the priest receives each species separately; then he pours the hosts (small cubes) into the chalice; each communicant receives a Host moistened in the Precious Blood. If the head is held back correctly, the mouth well open and the tongue left flat in the mouth, the priest can insert the little spoon, turn it over, and remove it without touching the teeth or tongue or lips of the communicant.

Can Roman Catholics receive Holy Communion according to the Byzantine rite? Yes, for Canon 866 of the Code of Canon Law says that you may receive Holy Communion according to any Catholic rite — "for the sake of piety."

THE BYZANTINE MASS

Rite of Preparations

Mass in the Byzantine rite, called the Holy Liturgy, begins with the preparation of the bread and wine by the priest at a small altar to the left of the sanctuary. This rite of preparation is called the *Proskomidia.* The bread and wine, when ready for Mass, are called the holy gifts.

The priest arranges the cubes of bread on the paten in a prescribed order: the large host in the center represents our Lord; a small host is placed on one side of the large one in honor of our Lady; nine small ones are placed on the other side in honor of the various classes of saints and recall by their number the nine choirs of angels. Then two rows of hosts placed below the large host commemorate the living and the dead. Thus, if the priest wishes to make a special commemoration for someone at the Liturgy, he places a small particle on the paten with a little prayer: "Remember, O Lord, Your servant *N...*" If such a one is deceased he says, "Be mindful, O Lord, of Your departed servant *N...*" This is a beautiful feature of the Byzantine rite — making physically present in the Mass each special memento.

When the gifts have been prepared and covered with veils, the priest incenses them and says a prayer of offering over them. This private beginning of the liturgy at the side altar commemorates the infancy and the hidden life of our Lord.

Public Liturgy

The celebrant now goes to the high altar to begin the public liturgy and this recalls the beginning of our Lord's public life of preaching and teaching and prayer. The priest begins by incensing the altar and sanctuary and people — a kind of sanctification to prepare them to assist at the sacred service.

The Great Litany

The great litany is sung, containing many general petitions for the good of mankind — for peace, for the Church, the hierarchy and rulers, for travelers, for the sick and suffering and imprisoned, for good weather, for the salvation of our souls. The priest keeps calling on the faithful to pray for various intentions and the answer of the people (and/or choir) is always the same: *Hospody pomiluy* or *Kyrie eleison* (Lord, have mercy).

There is something very beautiful about this form of litany prayer. Each petition is made with the general plea: "Lord, have mercy." We do not presume to tell God what to do nor how to do it; in each need we trust His merciful Providence; the best of us are but poor sinners before the throne of His mercy.

The great litany, as well as all the other small ones during the Mass, end with the touching formula:

Having commemorated our most holy, most pure, most blessed and glorious Lady, the Mother of God and ever-virgin Mary, together with all the Saints, let us commend ourselves, one another and our whole life to Christ our God.

The people answer: "To You, O Lord."

Three Antiphons

Three antiphons are sung by the choir, interspersed with the short litany. Along with the second antiphon the noble hymn of the Incarnation is sung:

O only-begotten Son and Word of God, although You are immortal, You condescended for our salvation to take flesh from the holy Mother of God and ever-Virgin Mary. Without undergoing change You became man. You were crucified, Christ God, by Your death trampling upon death. You who are one of the Holy Trinity and are glorified with the Father and the Holy Ghost, save us.

Toward the end of the third antiphon the priest picks up the large ornamented Gospel-Book which lies on the altar, and preceded by torch-bearers walks around the altar and out to the front of the sanctuary. This reminds us that Christ still lives and moves among us by His teaching.

Returning to the altar, he deposits the Gospel-Book in its usual place and the choir sings the anthem-prayers proper to that day or feast. This is followed by the solemn rendition of the Trisagion, the favorite hymn of the Eastern Churches: "Holy God, Holy Strong One, Holy Immortal One, have mercy on us!" This is repeated three times with the minor doxology (Glory be to the Father, etc.) inserted.

The Epistle and Gospel

Now follow the Epistle, the Alleluias and their versicles, and the Gospel. These all vary with the feast or Mass of the day. During the Alleluias the priest again does a complete incensation to prepare for the Gospel. The Gospel is sung facing the people, from the center of the sanctuary, and the acolytes stand beside the Book with lighted candles.

The Litanies

After the Gospel, if there is to be no sermon, litany prayers are again sung. A special litany is added for the catechumens, who are then ritually dismissed. The formula of dismissal is still sung, though they no longer have to leave the church.

Mass of the Faithful

Two more short litanies with two prayers for the faithful now follow, and it is time for the sacrifice proper to begin.

As the priest reads a long and beautiful prayer to prepare his own soul, the choir and people prepare theirs by singing the famed Hymn of the Cherubim: "Let us who here mystically represent the Cherubim in singing the thrice-holy hymn to the life-giving Trinity, let us now lay aside every earthly care . . . so that we may welcome the King of the Universe who comes escorted by invisible armies of angels. Alleluia, Alleluia, Alleluia!"

Altar, sanctuary, people are again incensed, and then priest and ministers go to the side altar to bring the holy gifts to the main altar. Lights and incense make this procession solemn, for it represents the triumphal entry of our Lord into Jerusalem and the beginning of Holy Week and the Passion which is about to be renewed in the holy sacrifice.

Now follows rapidly the offertory litany and prayers, the singing of the Nicene Creed, the preface and Sanctus, and the consecration.

The words of consecration are sung aloud and the people answer "Amen" to each formula. All the commemorations — of the saints, of the living, and of the dead — are made after the consecration.

The commemoration of our Lady is solemnly sung and is particularly beautiful. The usual form is:

It is indeed fitting to glorify you who brought forth God, forever blessed and completely spotless and the Mother of our God. Higher in honor than the Cherubim and incomparably more glorious than the Seraphim, who without harm to your virginity gave birth to the Word of God: you do we extol, true Mother of God!

The commemoration for the hierarchy is likewise sung aloud by the priest; a litany of petition is sung; the Our Father is chanted by priest and people together and it is time for Communion.

After Communion the priest blesses the people with what remains of the sacred species in the chalice. There is thus a Benediction of the Blessed Sacrament in every liturgy. This blessing recalls our Lord's blessing of the apostles after His Resurrection. Then the Blessed Sacrament is again incensed and carried back to the side altar, representing our Lord's Ascension into heaven.

Prayers of thanksgiving are said, the priest's blessing imparted, and the variable formula of dismissal is sung. Then the priest goes to the side altar, consumes what remains in the chalice and purifies the sacred vessels.

Many other small points of ceremonial could be explained, but this general outline will be sufficient to show the format of the Byzantine liturgy and to give at least a taste, in the passages quoted, of the treasures of poetic beauty and glorious prayer to be found there.

CHAPTER 3

EASTERN LAWS AND CUSTOMS

Eastern Christians, like those of the West, have certain laws and customs by which they live out their faith. Attendance at Church service on Sundays and holydays, observance of fast days, reception of the sacraments at Easter time — these distinguish both Catholic and Orthodox practice.

The Eastern calendar of feasts and fasts differs somewhat from the Western one. Many feasts of course are common to both, such as Christmas, Epiphany, Easter, Pentecost and the Assumption. Some saints' days are solemnized in East and West, such as St. John the Baptist (June 24) and Sts. Peter and Paul (June 29). The East celebrates also St. Nicholas (December 6), St. George (April 23) and Our Lady's Protection (October 1). The Annunciation (March 25) and Our Lady's Presentation (November 21), as well as her Nativity (September 8) are observed by both.

Fasting in the East has consisted usually of abstinence rather than the Western idea of only one full meal a day. In the United States and most of

Europe, Roman Catholics today observe abstinence (no meat may be eaten) on the Fridays of Lent and also fasting on Ash Wednesday and Good Friday. Christians in the Eastern rites observe strict fast on the first Monday of Lent and on Good Friday and Holy Saturday. Strict fast in the East prohibits the use of any foods that come from animals. This rules out eggs, milk, cheese, butter, as well as flesh meat itself. And yet cooks in the East, despite these severe restrictions, showed their skill by preparing savory dishes like holuptsi (cabbage leaves — in the near East, grape leaves — stuffed with rice flavored with onions sautéed in vegetable oil) and pirohi (dough patties stuffed with mashed potato seasoned with herbs and boiled). Nuts and fruits, vegetables and herbs, a variety of grains made for meals that were satisfying — although the restrictions of law gave also ample opportunity for mortification. Byzantine Christians of the Near East, like the Catholic Melchites, observe fasting by abstaining from all food from midnight until midday.

Perhaps the most striking difference of law and custom between East and West has to do with married clergy. Married men are ordained to the priesthood. Bishops must be celibate — often chosen from among priest-monks or widowers. If a priest's wife dies, he cannot marry again. The choice — either for marriage or for celibacy — has to be made before ordination to the diaconate.

In the early days of the Church, the apostles ordained married men even to the episcopate. St. Paul, for example, in his first Epistle to his disciple St. Timothy, bishop of Ephesus, tells him what qualities to look for in a man whom he wants to ordain a bishop. Among other things he says: "It behoveth therefore a bishop to be blameless, the husband of one wife." This means he must be a man who has not been married more than once, even though legitimately. The point we are making here is that St. Paul allowed the consecration of married men as bishops.

That the apostles often ordained married men is readily understandable when we realize that in choosing one of their new converts in some town to be the head of the new Christian community there, they would not pick some unmarried youth, but a man of mature years, prudent, of good reputation. Most men of this type would be married and fathers of families.

The ideal of celibacy was always cherished in the Church, although the apostles themselves (except St. John and St. Paul) were probably married men. St. Peter surely was, because our Lord cured his mother-in-law of a fever. St. Paul says that celibacy is the better thing for one who wishes to serve God: because if a man has a wife, he must be occupied to some extent, at least, with pleasing her, instead of being wholly intent upon the things of God. (I Cor. 7, 32).

This, then, was the condition in the early Church: both celibate and married clergy existed lawfully. In the Western Church celibacy gradually became the law. In the East celibacy became the law only for the bishops, but not for the priests, who could choose either marriage or celibacy. Monks of course were always celibate. These laws have remained in force down to the present day.

Since 1929, through a ruling of the Holy See, no more candidates for the priesthood may opt for marriage among the Eastern Catholics in the United States and Canada. The older married priests, of course, are still in good standing and after the second World War, many married Catholic priests accompanied their laity as refugees from Communist-Eastern Europe to the United States and Canada. These too, of course, are in good standing.

The question of introducing optional celibacy among Roman Catholic priests is often debated today. Some Catholics are very opposed to the idea of a married clergy, maintaining that the celibate ones are more ascetical. Eastern Christians will counter this by saying that their married priests are more fatherly. It is amusing that the same people who say they would not like to confide in a married priest find no trouble at all in telling very secret things to their doctors and lawyers.

The present author, teaching collegians, took a poll recently on student opinion (ages 20-22) about optional celibacy. There was no preparatory discussion; each one's personal ideas were requested. The overwhelming majority said that celibacy should be optional, usually for reasons such as: that this is something so personal in every life that no one except the person himself should have the choice; that marriage was something so good in itself, shielding a man at least somewhat against the awful loneliness of life, that it was needlessly cruel to deprive him of it; that marriage after all is a sacrament and its graces should help a priest spiritually; that if Christ himself did not demand celibacy of His followers, then no one else should presume to do so either. Many of today's psychologists and sociologists would underwrite these reasons and clerical associations are emphasizing in ever louder voices that at least the freedom of option be given to all priests.

If the present mandatory celibacy is ever relaxed for Western-Catholic clergy, the laity can still exercise their options of confessing either to a celibate or to a married priest, for both disciplines would continue to flourish. The laity can choose their confessors even now, for that matter, because Canon 905 allows any Catholic to confess to any authorized priest in any rite.

Holiness and zeal are not determined by celibacy or by marriage. Der Gomidas Keumurgian, a married Armenian priest of Constantinople, has been raised to the honors of the altar in St. Peter's in Rome because he died a martyr for his Catholic faith. Many married Catholic priests of Byzantine rite in Rumania and in the Ukraine suffered persecution and a few died for their faith at the hands of the Communists. On the other hand, psychotic and luxury-loving celibate priests have sometimes driven people away from religion because of their selfishness. All we can say in summation is: face the facts. Marriage for the clergy *has* worked in the East for almost twenty centuries. Dedicated service to God can be given by a celibate and by a married clergy. It depends on each individual's cooperation with grace and fidelity to prayer and work.

In 1966, in *Proche-Orient Chrétien* (XVI 4) a study was published by Robert Clément on the status of the married clergy in the Levant. This was then translated into English and appeared in the *Eastern Churches Review* (Vol. 1, 4 and Vol. II, 1); it was entitled "The Life of the Married Eastern Clergy."

Most married priests in the Near East are village priests, serving the country people. A large majority of the faithful in the rural districts are completely unwilling to have a pastor who is not married. Many vocations, not only to the married priesthood, but also to the religious life and the celibate-clerical ranks, come from the families of priests. This is true for Catholics and Orthodox alike.

Père Clément's study cites the eloquent words of the Maronite patriarch, Cardinal Paul-Peter Meouchi; "Liberty itself would decide the choice between celibacy and marriage . . . Should one leave whole areas without priests because one is unwilling

35

to agree to the marriage of a clergy which, to speak only for ourselves (i.e. the Maronite Catholics), has rendered appreciable services in the past for the salvation of souls, and still does so today?"

The Canon Law Society of America (CLSA) this year (1971) appointed a commission to study the question of clerical celibacy in today's world. The eighteen members of this commission, meeting in Douglastown, New York, issued a 14 page report entitled: *The Future Discipline of Priestly Celibacy.*

The Commission says it is not aiming to do away with celibacy, but merely to explore the reasonableness of allowing a married priesthood also to give its own type of witness to the Gospel.

Local bishops should be the ones to judge how many and which married men are to be ordained. The married clergy are to enjoy equal status with the celibates within the Church.

The Eastern-rite Catholics throughout the world are urged to return completely to their age-old custom of ordaining married men.

The CLSA also recommended that the present canon law imposing a diriment matrimonial impediment on those in Sacred Orders be removed. They also think that if a priest wishes to resign from the ministry, this permission should be granted him by his local (diocesan) authorities, removing the present necessity of having to appeal each case to Rome, which procedure in the past caused a great deal of delay for — with resultant anguish to — the petitioner.

Recommendations, similar to these made by the Canon Law Society of America, are becoming constantly more common as a result of the deliberations of priests' councils throughout the Catholic world.

It may well be that in this instance, too, the Western Church has much to learn from the East.

CHAPTER 4

BYZANTINE ART AND MUSIC

Art

The past 30 years have seen a great change in the artistic taste of Western Christians. In a gradual reaction against the saccharine glamour of prettified Christs and Hollywood-starlet Madonnas, the stern majesty of Byzantine iconography has come to impress and win the affection of a large public.

Two factors have aided immensely in accomplishing this result:

1. The dispersal of numerous Eastern rite Christians, both Catholics and Orthodox, throughout Western Europe and the Americas.

2. The extraordinary spread throughout the world of devotion to our Lady of Perpetual Help, whose miraculous image is an icon of finest Byzantine culture.

Byzantine art spread throughout the Greek empire and was long popular in Italy as the mosaic work in the oldest Italian churches amply demonstrates. The interiors of Byzantine churches glory in a multitude of sacred pictures (icons).

At one time Moslem-inspired attacks upon the icons threatened their continued existence both as an art form and as devotional aids. But Byzantine tradition overcame the iconoclasts ("image-breakers"); and, sanctioned by the Seventh Ecumenical Council held at Nice in 787, veneration of the holy pictures developed so swiftly, that their sacred presence, in profusion, in Byzantine churches, is a characteristic of that church's artistic image.

The custom then arose, too, of separating the sanctuary or "holy of holies" from the nave of the church by erecting a screen pierced by three doors. On this screen, covered with an array of pictures, certain icons must appear. To the right of the double-central doors is the large icon of our Lord. To the left is the Mother of God, Infant in arms. Above the central doors is the Last Supper, and stretching out on both sides from this icon are the pictures of the chief feasts of the year — such as the Resurrection, the Ascension, the Nativity, etc.

On the central doors there will usually appear the scene of the Annunciation — our Lady kneeling on the right door and St. Gabriel the Archangel standing on the left. The two lateral or "diaconal" doors will usually have images of the Protodeacons St. Stephen and St. Lawrence. To the side of these one will ordinarily find special saints such as the patron of the church on one side and St. Nicholas on the other.

These images not only remind an Eastern Christian of the saint or scene depicted but also, in some mysterious way, manifest the presence of the holy ones shown. Thus the images receive more constant veneration than usually happens in the West, with lamps and candles burning before them and the tribute of incense paid to them at every church service.

The Byzantine icons are highly stylized and

conventional. Neither strict perspective nor perfect symmetry are considered necessary. The bodies are usually very thin and the faces tend to be gaunt — in accord with Eastern monasticism's ideals of holiness — for through the centuries the monks, like those of Mt. Athos, have made iconography one of their chief avocations. More modern Greek and Ukrainian iconography tends to greater realism and naturalism in the faces, but the Russian school continues gaunt and severe.

All of the pictures produce a dramatic effect of solemnity and devotion. A great deal of gold is used in coloring the icons and very often the whole background is of gold; this represents the richness of heaven. Many of the famous icons, especially Madonnas, venerated in the cathedrals and great monasteries were simply encrusted with gold, leaving only the face and hands of the original painting uncovered. Our Lady and the Infant are often crowned with precious golden diadems heavy with jewels.

Since many of the figures in iconography, especially among the saints, look so similar, the custom arose of marking next to the saints, usually beside the head, the abbreviations of the name. Often the whole name is given, and the letters are remarkably mingled together.

Sometimes an icon, like that of our Lady of Perpetual Help, will tell a story in the one picture. The Infant Lord is clasping His Mother's right hand with both of His and looking apprehensively behind Him. One of His sandals is hanging loose by one thong. The legend: one day the child Jesus, frightened by a vision of the instruments of His future Passion carried by two angels, runs to His Mother in such speed and alarm that one sandal comes loose. Our Lady picks Him up and He reposes upon her left arm, while He clutches her right hand with both

His tiny hands, looking back at the angels.

Music

The music used in the Byzantine rite varies greatly from country to country. The Greeks employ a chant that is based on the ancient Greek modes, but which is now very enharmonic, that is, many intervals other than the old diatonic scales' whole tones and halftones are used, e.g., quarter and eighth tones. The result to Western ears is at first unpleasant, and sounds like repetitious crying and wailing. After a while one becomes used to this and recognizes the ethereal beauty of some of the phrases and the emotional coloring given to certain words of the text. Some of the melodies yield to harmonization; others understandably do not.

An attractive feature of Greek chant is the "ison." One or more singers keep holding the tonic or bass note of the mode (scale-tonality) in which the piece is sung. If the mode changes in the course of the melody, the ison note will also change. The effect is fascinating, like that of the drone-pipe in bagpipe playing. The ison and the melody are constantly giving rise to consonance and dissonance. Traditionally, all Byzantine music is sung a cappella, though in recent years organs have been introduced into some churches, especially among the Greeks. But enharmonic melodies cannot be accompanied on an instrument made to play only diatonic intervals. The emerging practice of playing the nearest diatonic note on the organ and letting the voices slide and slither through the lesser intervals simply destroys the melodies' charm and finesse. It makes both organ and voices sound off pitch.

The Slav churches of Byzantine rite follow their own system of tones which are diatonic, but not modal in the Gregorian or Greek sense of the word. The people often harmonize the melodies with considerable skill, and the choirs sing harmony and polyphony of the 18th century Western-European style. Ruthenian and Ukrainian music is more melodic than the Russian, but the Russian style, achieving maximum development in the 19th century, is very serious and devotional and appeals to most Western ears at once. Great Russian composers like Rimsky-Korsakov and Gretchaninov devoted their energies to harmonizing existing church chants and developing new music in the same reverential vein.

Ukrainian and Russian church choirs produce some of the finest choral music to be heard anywhere in the world and, often enough, first-class music will be produced Sunday after Sunday in churches modest in size and resources.

CHAPTER 5

DEVELOPMENT OF EÁSTERN ORTHODOX THEOLOGY

Schism between East and West

Though some Church historians term July 16, 1054 the most lamentable date in Church history, it would be a mistake to suppose that on July 15, 1054 there was one undivided Church and on July 17 there was an accomplished schism between East and West.

The forces alienating East and West were already operative in the fourth century: Constantine moved his capital from Rome to Byzantium. Knowledge of Latin became rare in the East, and Greek was soon completely eclipsed by Latin in the West. Communications were never ideal. When pope and patriarch wished to exchange letters, the documents had to be entrusted to paid emissaries: it would be still many centuries before the emergence of a postal system in the world.

There were several short periods of schism between Rome and Constantinople before the 11th century, the most noteworthy occurring during the patriarchate of Photius in the ninth century. During this period of disunion, Photius composed an encyclical letter which he sent to the bishops in the East complaining about the the errors of the Latins — he mentions fasting on Saturday, clerical celibacy, reserving Confirmation to bishops, using dairy products during the first week of Lent as well as the more serious matters of the addition of the *Filioque* to the Creed (teaching that the Holy Spirit proceeds from the Father and the Son) and the primacy of the pope.

Peace and reunion were restored after the Photian schism, but to what extent the climate of anti-Latinism was being established can be inferred from the fact that 150 years after the death of Photius, the Patriarch Michael Caerularius attacked the Latins, and the catalogue of "abuses" had grown from Photius' seven to an alarming list of 22. Among these are seriously listed such petty objections to divergent discipline as shaving clerics, monks eating meat, bishops wearing rings, etc.

It is true that theological development was different in East and West. The East was always more mystical, more patristic; it more penetratingly linked up every feature of religion with the divine economy of salvation. The West was more practical, dynamic, precise in formulation, rigidly logical in distinctions, ready to determine how far everyone *had* to go in belief and practice rather than viewing in rapture how far a saint *might* advance toward the ideal. The West measured obligations; the East envisioned man's divinization corresponding to the Logos' humanization in the Incarnation.

Both East and West could have taught each other very much. Each side suffered from the schism and from being cut off from the other's kind of theological development.

PERIODS OF THEOLOGICAL DEVELOPMENT

There are seven periods of theological movement in the East which are readily distinguished.

1. Philosophical-Patristic Period

The first period, from the 9th to the 14th century, is called the Philosophical-Patristic period. Michael Psellos and John Italus are the philosophers most praised. Plato and Aristotle are the guides. Euthymius Zigabenus (chief commentator on Sacred Scripture), Nicetas Stethatos (chief monastic author of the period and dogmatician), and John Bekkos (chief apologist) are the names that dominate this era. Bekkos was patriarch of Constantinople and attended the Reunion Council of Lyon in 1274. When he returned to Constantinople he eloquently defended the Latins' *Filoque* as being the equivalent of the Eastern Fathers "from the Father through the Son." He died in union with the Western Church.

2. Scholastic Period

The second period, from the 14th to the 16th century, is called the Scholastic Period. It is characterized by the influence of St. Thomas' thought. His works were translated into Greek by Demetrios Kydonios and his brother Prochorus. Demetrios was the Latin secretary to the emperor. The Greeks eagerly read and studied St. Thomas, but steadfastly refused to believe that a work of such theological refinement could have been produced in the "barbaric West which is given over only to grosser avocations like hunting and soldiering." The Kydonios brothers vigorously defended the honor of St. Thomas. Georgios Scholarios also distinguished himself by his devotion to St. Thomas.

3. Reformation Period

The third period, from the 16th to the 17th century, is the Reformation period and is characterized by a reaction against the positions of the Protestants.

When the Lutherans at the University of Tübingen appealed to the Greek Patriarch asking for recognition as a fellow antipapal Church, Jeremias II sent them a long letter, in 1576, in which he outlines the many features that fundamentally separate the Orthodox Church from Protestantism.

When Cyril Lukaris became Patriarch of Constantinople he espoused Protestant tenets such as declaring Sacred Scripture the sole rule of faith. As a result he was condemned by two Orthodox synods, one held at Jassy in Rumania in 1642 and the other at Jerusalem in 1672. This period is famous also for the production of several "symbolic books" and for the establishment of a theological school at Kiev in 1631 by the Metropolitan Peter Moghila, in which Thomism was taught and the language of instruction was Latin.

4. Eighteenth Century Protestant Influences

The fourth period, the 18th century, is marked by an influx of Protestant ideas into Russian theology. This was caused by Theophanes Prokopovich, Bishop of Pskov, afterward Metropolitan of Novgorod. He was a political opportunist and a court favorite. In servile flattery to the emperor he dared to apply Christ's words to St. Peter to Tsar Peter the Great: "Thou are Peter and upon this rock I shall build my church." He espoused Protestant views on justification, the canon of Sacred Scripture, Scripture as the sole rule of faith, etc. Philaret Drozhdov, Metropolitan of Moscow, published two catechisms enshrining the errors of Prokopovich.

5. Nineteenth Century Orthodox Reaction

The fifth period, the 19th century, marks a return to Orthodox positions in a reaction against the influence of Prokopovich. Nicholas Protasoff, the lay procurator of the Holy Synod, spearheaded the reform. He corrected the worst errors in Phil-aret's catechisms. The renewed Orthodoxy also appeared in the theological manuals of Makarios Bulgakoff.

6. Modern Era

The sixth period is the modern era and embraces the latter 19th and the 20th centuries. Probably the chief characteristics of this period have been the emergence of the Slavophiles and their idealistic concept of the Church of Christ.

German idealistic philosophy made great head-way in Russia, especially that of Kant, Fichte and Schelling. The Slavophiles stressed "feeling" in reli-gion, knowing God by personal experience, union of believers in love, and decried organization in the Church. The most influential among them are: John Kirievsky, Alexios Khomiakov, and Vladimir Soloviev. The last named became a Catholic.

7. Modernism

It must also be admitted that to some extent Modernism made some inroads into Orthodoxy, especially in the theological schools of Paris (Russian Orthodox emigres) and Athens (Greek). Modern Orthodox theologians tend to magnify the concept of passivity because they claim that God can and does do everything. They tend to overlook secondary causality — the use of human instru-ments — which is also of divine institution. The same Lord who said "I say to you that God is able out of these stones to raise up children to Abra-ham" (Matt. 3, 9) also said: "Go into the whole world and preach the Gospel to every creature" (Mark 16, 15).

The Protestant theologian Ritschl accuses the Orthodox of "liturgicality." By this he means that the Orthodox rely excessively on liturgical practice as an ultimate source of truth. The Catholic histo-rian Jugie accuses the Orthodox of "traditionalism."

By this he means that the Orthodox tend to regard everything they have and do as absolutely perfect and hence resist any least change in even the minutest accidents of practice and discipline.

The West in general accuses the East of being static — "grown stiff in gold and brocade." The East accuses the West in turn of excessive legalism and rationalism and irreverent proneness to change things around — "inventing new dogmas" and discipline, ignoring tradition, etc. Obviously, nothing is accomplished by name-calling.

Fasting

It is interesting to compare just one discipline in the three great Christian bodies: fasting. Protestants in general do away with all fasting and abstinence. Catholics have liberalized the ancient laws, long preserving abstinence on Fridays (but now dispensing from it generally) and some simple and observable laws of fasting. The Orthodox still maintain, officially, the ancient fast and periods and techniques of the early Church. Several times the Patriarch of Constantinople has attempted to mitigate and modernize the fasting laws. This aroused such a furor that he desisted. In the meantime not many Orthodox abroad observe the fasting and abstinence laws; but they resist changing them.

On the other hand, many humble folk in Orthodox lands observe the fasting just as religiously as any feature of their religion. Palmer, in his book, *Notes on a Visit to the Russian Church 1839-40*, tells of a traveler, a German Lutheran, who was journeying from Petrograd to Archangel. He came to a small village at nightfall. There was no hotel. He approached the largest house and asked to stay. He was invited in with Christian hospitality and was asked to share the evening meal.

It was great Lent: the menu consisted of black

bread and tea. The traveler went to his pack and brought out some cooked pork. The Russians were horrified to see him eat some of it with his bread. One of them, coming up behind the German, split open his head with an ax for daring to flout the Lenten observance. Under German diplomatic pressure the Russian government sent the Russian to Siberia, but to all the villagers he was a great hero who had fought for the purity of Orthodoxy.

Great Orthodox bishops, like Metrophanes Azofsky of Veronezh and Patriarch Dositheos of Jerusalem, have summed up their dying legacy to their flocks in the terse phrase: "Resist unto death every least change!"

Theology and Passivity

Orthodox theologians do not readily employ our Western divisions of dogmatic, moral, ascetical and mystical theology. For that matter, these distinctions were not current in the West either until the last two or three hundred years.

Eugene Popov's book on *Russian Religious Practice* devotes a chapter to proper veneration of icons. What with us would be merely an adjunct of devotion or an expression of piety becomes for an Orthodox believer a necessary expression of his faith.

The attitude of passivity is a strong undercurrent in Eastern theology. Even the sacramental formulas tend to express this: "The servant of God *N* is baptized in the name of the Father, etc."; the servant of God *N* is communicated with the honorable and holy body and blood, etc." Comparatively little foreign missionary work has been done, leaving all to the Providence of God. Contemplative religious are important to the Church to grow in personal holiness, not to become active religious busy in the world. The transubstantiation in the liturgy is effected by the operation of the Holy Spirit rather than by the priest's enunciation of the words of consecration, etc.

The traditional Catholic attitude toward all this has been summed up as follows: pray as if everything depended on God; work as if everything depended on you.

Interest in, and understanding of, Orthodox-theological viewpoints have been aided immensely in recent years by the appearance of well-written books in English. These have had as their authors chiefly the very capable professors of St. Vladimir's Orthodox Seminary near New York City. The names of Alexander Schmemann, John Meyendorff, and Nicholas Arseniev are now well known. Their works will be found listed in the bibliography at the end of this book.

Orthodox Theological Books

It is seldom possible to say absolutely: such and such is the teaching of Orthodox theologians. Why? Because on every point there is a large variety of opinion — all the way up to full Catholic dogma and all the way down to Protestant modernism.

Surely the last statement is an exaggeration; surely no Orthodox theologian holds the papal primacy! Yet Vassili Rosanov, in his book, *Along the Walls of the Church*, published in St. Petersburgh in 1906 writes:

"The words of Christ, 'feed my lambs, feed my sheep' contain the whole doctrine of the papacy, which follows certainly as a corollary from them. Our theologians do not know how to explain them, except to keep repeating like parrots: 'All the apostles are equal; no one is greater than the others.' That is why the Bishop of Rome is equal only to the Bishop of Koluga! (Koluga is a little town near Moscow.) How such arguments are repugnant to

Russian honesty! Say rather about these words in the Gospel: 'I don't understand them' or rather 'I understand them, but I don't want to admit them!' "

Later on Rosanov goes on to say: "The Pope has received all Peter's primacy from our Lord himself. But I am a Russian. I am an Orthodox. And so I reject the papacy. But I have not lost my logic — and with that I declare: The pope is the rock on which the whole Church depends and he is pastor of the whole flock. Apart from him there is only babbling."

However, despite many varieties of opinion on individual points, the general teaching of the Orthodox is that which is found in their official sources.

Official Source of Theology

Orthodox agree with Catholics that there is a dual Rule of Faith: Sacred Scripture and Tradition.

The Greeks hold the same Canon of Sacred Scripture as the Catholics and for the Old Testament they follow the Septuagint.

The Russians are divided, some of them rejecting the so-called deuterocanonical books of the Old Testament. These are Wisdom, Baruch, Ecclesiasticus, Machabees I and II, Tobias, Judith, parts of Esther and Daniel. This confusion dates from the protestantizing of Prokopovich and is found in Philaret Drozhdov's Catechism. When Protasoff expunged the non-Orthodox errors from the Catechism, he strangely overlooked this one.

Tradition is found enshrined in the same sources used by Catholics, namely, the writings of the Fathers of the Church and the decrees of the Councils. But the Orthodox acknowledge only the first seven Ecumenical Councils and declare that their decrees are to be received and venerated like the Gospels themselves.

The Nicene Creed is the one universally accepted and recited in all liturgical functions. The Apostles' Creed is rarely found among them; the Athanasian Creed is not much used.

Of great authority among the Orthodox are also the books which they call the "Symbolic Books." *Symbolon* is the Greek word for creed; these books therefore are so authoritative that they resemble creeds. They are acknowledged generally as true summations of Orthodox belief.

Symbolic Books

1. Metropolitan Peter Moghila's *Confessio Fidei Orthodoxae* published in Latin in 1640. The Greeks use a modified version of it edited by Meletios Syrigos.

2. *The Confession of Dositheos* by the Patriarch Dositheos of Jerusalem, who was anxious to preserve his flock from the "errors" of both Catholicism and Protestantism. His work was greatly praised by the Orthodox Council of Jerusalem in 1672.

3. Metropolitan Philaret Droxhdov's Catechisms, published in Moscow in 1823 and 1827 and finally in de-protestantized form in 1839.

Regarded as sources of quasi-symbolic nature are the:

1. Response of Patriarch Jeremias II to the Lutheran theologians in 1576, restating the points on which Orthodox belief differed from that of the Reformers.

2. The Encylical Letter of Patriarch Anthimos VI in 1895, rejecting the invitation to Church Unity of Pope Leo XIII.

For Catholic students studying Orthodox theology there is the monumental reference work of Martin Jugie, A.A. (Paris 1926) entitled *Theologia Dogmatica Christianorum Orientalium ab Ecclesias*

Catholica Dissendentium (4 Vols.).

Useful handbooks are those of Father Maurice Gordillo, S.J., *Compendium Theologiae Orientalis* (Rome, 2 edit. 1939) and Father Nicholas Ladomerszky's *Theologia Orientalis* (Rome 1953).

Selected articles appear in the periodicals *Irenikon, Stoudion, Echos d'Orient, Orientalia Christiana, Eastern Churches Quarterly, The Ark, Diakonia.*

A fine over-all picture of the history of the divergencies between East and West is found in *Le Schisme Byzantin* by Father Jugie (Parish 1941).

For further references see the bibliography.

CHAPTER 6

SACRAMENTAL
THEOLOGY

Baptism

Baptism is the Christian rite of initiation. Until one has received Baptism he is incapable of receiving any other sacrament. For a thousand years, in East and West, Baptism was usually administered by immersion, that is, by dipping a person completely into a body of water. This symbolized his death to the past and his burial with Christ. Coming up out of the water, he was a new man and had experienced a spiritual resurrection.

This coincides with the imagery in St. Paul's words: "Do you not know that all we who have been baptized into Christ Jesus have been baptized into his death? For we were buried with him by means of Baptism into death, in order that, just as Christ has arisen from the dead through the glory of the Father, so we also may walk in newness of life" (Rom. 6:3-4).

However, even though Baptism by immersion was the *usual* type for hundreds of years, it was not the only type used, even from the beginning.

As a result of St. Peter's sermon preached in Jerusalem on the first Pentecost, 3,000 people entered the new Church. It is not probable that so many people could have received Baptism by immersion in water-shy Jerusalem in a single day. But we read in Acts 2:41: "Now they who received his word *were baptized*, and there were added *that day* about 3,000 souls."

On the second missionary journey, St. Paul at Philippi baptized the jailer and his household on the night of the earthquake (Acts 16:33). It is not likely that facilities were available in the jail for Baptism by immersion.

Probably one of the oldest extra-Scriptural documents that we have (60-100 A.D.), *The Didache*, expressly mentions that if one does not have "living water" (the running water of a stream for immersion), it will suffice to pour water on the forehead three times as one recites the words of Baptism.

It is true that St. Paul's symbolism of death and resurrection is more graphically portrayed through Baptism by immersion; but it is not true to say that a Baptism is invalid simply because an accidental symbolism is not portrayed. The Orthodox themselves sometimes administered Baptism by infusion (pouring), especially in emergencies and particularly in Russia, where many months of cold rendered Baptism by immersion impractical.

Regarding repetition of Baptism when Catholics joined the Orthodox Church, there has been no consistency of practice. The Russians rebaptized Catholics from 1620 to 1667. The Greeks did so from 1755 to 1875. In 1880 it was decreed at Constantinople that no Latins, Armenians or Protestants were to be rebaptized when they joined the Orthodox Church.

The basic reasoning behind the rebaptizing was

this: all sacraments administered by one who did not possess the true Orthodox faith were invalid. If occasionally the Orthodox Church accepted non-Orthodox sacraments without repeating them, it was through an application of the principle of "economy." In this case the Orthodox Church applied to a soul the grace without the performance of the sacramental rite.

Sometimes Orthodox clergy repeat the Baptism because they know that the Catholic clergy repeat the Baptism of Orthodox entering the Catholic Church. Of course we know that these Catholic priests baptize conditionally; but the Orthodox clergy do not know this and resent it bitterly. One of my classmates at the Pontifical Oriental Institute in Rome, a Friar Minor who had spent some years working in Egypt, assured me that hundreds of Coptic Christians refused to become Catholics because the Catholic authorities there ordered conditional rebaptism.

One cannot help sympathizing with Orthodox feeling in this regard, for two reasons:

1. The Holy See has repeatedly acknowledged the validity of Orthodox sacraments.

2. Catholic theologians acknowledge the validity of emergency Baptisms administered even by atheists if they have at least the intention "of doing what the Church does," as the Council of Trent phrased it.

Hence, the reason for conditional rebaptism sometimes adduced by Catholic chanceries that "maybe the Orthodox ministrant did not have the right intention," sounds a bit hollow in Orthodox ears.

The Orthodox do not accept the Baptism administered by an unbeliever. The minister must be at least a believing Christian himself, even though, as in some cases, the minister is heretical. This represents the common Orthodox opinion today.

Confirmation

The indelible character of Confirmation is not usually held by the Orthodox, and so they generally reconfirm converts from Catholicism. Sometimes they reconfirm people who were originally confirmed as Orthodox, then fell away from the Orthodox faith, and later want to return to it.

The Orthodox polemicists attack the Western practice of reserving Confirmation to the bishop. But in this connection it is to be noted that the Orthodox themselves allow the priest to use for Confirmation only chrism that has been consecrated by a bishop, whereas in administering the sacrament of Extreme Unction, the oil is blessed by the priest as part of the ceremony.

Moreover, the West does not deny the validity of Confirmation administered by priests, and in fact permits this quite frequently. For example, the Catholic priests of the Byzantine rite administer the sacrament of Confirmation immediately after Baptism. The pope regularly gave permission to confirm to all cardinals that were priests (and not in bishop's orders), to abbots for their own subjects, to vicars and prefects apostolic that were not bishops, and often to priests in mission territory within which a bishop could not travel without grave inconvenience.

Finally, in 1946, Pope Pius XII granted permission to all pastors to confirm persons in danger of death in their territory, lest anyone die without the opportunity of strengthening his soul with this great sacrament.

Penance

Orthodox and Catholic theologians agree in their theoretical treatment of the sacrament of Penance.

However, there are some discrepancies in the Orthodox practice of confession which may be noted here.

In general, the Orthodox do not practice frequent confession as in the West. A good Orthodox confesses a few times a year, though he is bound, like a Catholic, to confess only once a year, at Easter time. (Strictly speaking, of course, a Catholic would not need to confess at Easter time if he had no serious sin to tell.)

There is a practice among some Orthodox of making merely generic accusations of sin or of merely answering the priest's questions by saying, "I am a sinner." Orthodox theological writers prescribe an exact accusation in theory; but in practice this is often neglected.

Among more recent Orthodox theologians there is a tendency to regard the penance or *epitimia* as something merely medicinal rather than satisfactory for the remission of temporal punishment due to sin. This view derives from Protestant influences stressing the fact that Christ's death made full satisfaction for all the sins of mankind.

It is true, of course, that our Lord's death made most perfect and universal satisfaction for sin; yet we may not ignore the teaching of Holy Scripture enjoining penance upon all adult Christians for their sins and in imitation of Christ's suffering.

Our Lord says: "If anyone wishes to come after me, let him deny himself and take up his cross and follow me" (Matt. 16:24). St. Peter tells the Christians of the early Church: "Christ also has suffered for you, leaving you an example that you may follow his steps" (1 Peter 2:21). And St. Paul is very clear in his warning that we must add our sufferings to those of the Church: "I rejoice now in the sufferings I bear for your sake; and what is lacking of the sufferings of Christ I fill up in my flesh for his body, which is the Church" (Coloss. 1:24).

In the Epistle to the Romans he writes: "If we are sons, we are heirs also: heirs indeed of God and joint heirs with Christ, provided, however, we suffer with him that we may also be glorified with him" (Rom. 8:17).

The Orthodox do not share the Catholic preoccupation with "jurisdiction," that is, permission from the local bishop or superior to hear confessions in his territory.

If an Orthodox priest is validly ordained and is in good standing in his own diocese, then he has jurisdiction to hear Orthodox believers' confessions anywhere in the world. This strikes the present author as most reasonable. In the foreseeable future there will be a liberalizing of jurisdiction among Catholics too. Some metropolitan areas, consisting of several dioceses, are already interchanging jurisdiction and in some places in Europe a priest has permission to confess penitents in the whole country if he has it in his own diocese.

Holy Orders

Not all Orthodox theologians agree in stating that Holy Orders imprints a character on the soul. But at the great Russian Synod held in Moscow in 1917-1918, the Fathers of the assembly clearly stated their belief that an indelible character is imprinted on the soul through Holy Orders. Some Orthodox who doubted this indelible character possibly did so as a result of Protestant influences, since the Reformers overstressed the character of Baptism as the great and only necessary sacrament.

The Anointing of the Sick

The proof from Sacred Scripture for the existence of this sacrament is found in St. James' Epistle

5, 14-15: "Is anyone among you sick? Let him bring in the priests of the Church, and let them pray over him, anointing him with oil in the name of the Lord. And the prayer of faith will save the sick man, and the Lord will raise him up, and if he be in sins, they shall be forgiven him."

Orthodox theologians make two objections to the Catholic use of "the Anointing."

1. We do wrongly to have it administered by one priest when St. James says "let him bring in the *priests* of the Church." The Orthodox claim seven priests should administer the sacrament.

2. Catholics have no right to limit the administration of this sacrament to one who is in danger of death, because St. James' statement makes no such limitation.

On both these points Catholic theologians invoke the practice of the Church as the legitimate interpretation of the text. In most cases the sacrament would never be given and thus, souls in need would be deprived of the grace Christ wishes them to have through it, since it is practically impossible to assemble seven priests in order to administer it.

Catholics understand "priests of the Church" to represent an appeal to the *priesthood* for this spiritual help — which then is given if one of them answers the call. A too scrupulous adherence to the ritual calling for seven priests has often resulted in a neglect of this sacrament among the Orthodox.

Regarding the danger of death, this seems to be at least implied in the words "the prayer of faith will save the sick man." How save him? Both physically and spiritually. He is spiritually saved by the remission of his sins. He is physically saved if he escapes death and recovers. Hence, some danger of death seems to be implied.

The ritual prayers in both East and West beg God to restore the sick person to health. In practice the

Russian Orthodox administer this sacrament only when there is a case of serious illness involving some danger of death. Among the Greeks, the practice has been introduced of anointing even those in good health who come forward to receive it — usually once a year during Holy Week.

Formerly this sacrament was called "Extreme Unction," literally, *last* anointing or anointing of one *"in extremis"* (actually dying). Today the Catholic Church prefers to call the sacrament simply the "Anointing of the Sick." Anyone who is seriously sick may ask for it. Serious sickness always involves some danger of death even though it be not immediate.

The blessing of the oil to be used for the sacrament can be performed by the Byzantine priest at the beginning of the ceremony and forms part of the prescribed ritual. In the new Catholic ritual this practice will be adapted for use in the revised liturgy of the Anointing of the Sick.

The Holy Eucharist (*The Epiclesis*)

The *Epiclesis* is the name given to the prayer in the Byzantine liturgy occurring soon after the consecration, in which the power of the Holy Spirit is invoked upon the Eucharistic elements. The text reads:

Moreover, we offer You this spiritual and bloodless sacrifice, and we pray and beseech and entreat You: send down Your Holy Spirit upon us and upon these gifts lying before us . . . and make this bread the precious body of Your Christ. Amen. And that which is in this chalice the precious Blood of Your Christ. Amen. Having changed them by Your Holy Spirit. Amen, Amen, Amen.

So that for those who receive them in Communion, they may serve as a cleansing for the soul, for the forgiveness of their sins, as a communication of the Holy Spirit and a full participation in the kingdom of heaven, and to promote their confidence in You — and let them not serve for the judgment or condemnation of any who receive them.

The question about the true meaning of the *Epiclesis* was first treated as a matter of controversy by Nicholas Cabasilas in the 14th century in his *Exposition of the Sacred Liturgy* (MG-155,729).

At the Council of Florence (1438) the matter was discussed, and all the Greeks except Mark of Ephesus and Isidore of Kiev admitted that it was the words of consecration (or *Institution*) which effected the transubstantiation. Mark of Ephesus claimed that the words of institution and the *Epiclesis* were equally important and necessary. Older Orthodox theologians follow him.

Some modern Greek theologians such as Androutsos and Dyobouniotes, say that only the *Epiclesis* effects the consecration. Most Slav authors hold that both the consecration and the *Epiclesis* are necessary.

Let us examine the arguments adduced by Orthodox theologians from the days of Nicholas Cabasilas until now. They say that the operation of each sacrament should be effected by an invocatory prayer. In the Mass it is done by invoking the Holy Spirit. Catholic theologians admit the operation of the Holy Spirit in all the sacraments, but deny that it has to be explicitly invoked in order to function.

Cabasilas maintains that the words of institution are not the apt form for the sacrament because they are not joined to the sign of the cross. Catholics say that the Eucharist is a unique sacrament by Christ's very institution; it is a sacrifice as well as a sacrament; it not only gives grace but contains the very Author of grace. Hence, it is not necessary that it parallel the other sacramental rites completely. However, the bread and wine *are blessed* with the sign of the cross before the words are said.

Cabasilas says that even the Latins, in practice, have an *Epiclesis* in their Mass, namely, in the prayer *Supplices te rogamus* after the consecration. Simeon of Thessalonica says the Latins have an *Epiclesis*, but before the consecration, namely, in the prayer *Quam oblationem*. Latin liturgists admit that there is some reason to look upon these prayers as being *Epicleses*, but only in an obscure way.

It is interesting to note that in the three new Canons of the Mass published for use in the Roman rite, each one has an explicit prayer to the Holy Spirit asking for the exercise of His sanctifying power.

Cabasilas says that in the liturgy of St. Basil, the sacred gifts are called *antitypa*, i.e., "species," after the consecration and just before the *Epiclesis* proper. Catholics reply that this word *antitypa* employed by St. Basil does not prove the saint did not yet consider the gifts consecrated, because the word is used by Greek Fathers even when there can be no doubt from the context that the real body and blood are meant.

St. Cyril of Jerusalem (MG 33, 1124) says: "Those who taste are not bidden to taste bread and wine, but the species (*antitypon*) of the Body and Blood of Christ." After the *Epiclesis* proper, St. Basil's liturgy prays that "we all who become partakers of this *one bread and chalice* may be united, etc."

Does this prove that even *after the Epiclesis* St. Basil denies the real presence just because he does not say "body and blood" instead of bread and chalice?

The Orthodox adduce St. John Damascene as support for their theory because he speaks of the importance and necessity of the *Epiclesis*. St. Thomas Aquinas, commenting on this point, declared (in IV sentent., 1, IV, dist., VIII, quaest. II, art. 3, and I): "The operation of the Holy Spirit as principal agent does not exclude the instrumental power of the Savior's words."

However, even if St. John Damascene's words cannot be explained by St. Thomas' distinction, then it is still possible to concede that on this point the great Damascene erred. Moreover, we should like to match St. John Damascene's assertion with the clear declaration of another great Eastern Doctor, St. John Chrysostom, who most clearly teaches that the words of institution effect the change (MG 49, 380): "The priest stands and says, 'This is my body.' This saying (*rhema*) transforms what lies before him."

Again, the very fact that the oldest codices of the Byzantine liturgy prescribe a deep bow from the clergy after the words of institution, and the solemnity with which the words are sung aloud and are answered with "Amen" by the people, is a proof that the ancients really considered the consecration as the moment when the transubstantiation took place. Moreover, in the Coptic and Ethiopian rites, the people not only sing "Amen" after the words of consecration, but they add phrases like "This is now indeed true; this we firmly believe, etc."

What then is the true sense of the *Epiclesis* prayer? How do Catholics explain it?

Catholic Doctrine of Epiclesis

There are two accepted theories. The first is that of Cardinal Bessarion, who declares that what happens at the moment of the consecration is something so stupendous that the liturgy can view it only in parts and can appreciate it only by degrees. Since all the activities of the Blessed Trinity outside itself are the results of cooperation of all three Persons, the consecration in the liturgy is also the work of all three Persons.

Now the liturgy stresses the work of the Father before the consecration (in the preface), the work of the Son during the consecration (in the account of the Institution), the work of the Holy Spirit after the consecration (in the *Epiclesis*). It happens in the other sacraments, too, e.g., Baptism and Anointing of the Sick, that the prayers said after the "form" ask for the graces already given in the sacrament that was just conferred when matter and form were united.

The second Catholic explanation of the *Epiclesis*, and the one favored at the Council of Florence, looks upon the prayer as a petition for the fruits of Communion, that these consecrated elements be made the instrument of grace for us when we receive them. Hence, the upholders of this theory say that the essential sense of the prayer is found in the second part where we read: "*So that* for those who receive them in Communion, they may serve as a cleansing for the soul, for the forgiveness of their sins, etc. . . . " Hence, the Holy Spirit's beneficent operation is invoked so that the fruits of Holy Communion may come to us.

Both these explanations have much to commend them and each of them serves to highlight very interesting truths about the liturgy.

Surely Catholics and Orthodox could find a ready formula of harmonization by agreeing that the elements are transformed during the great Eucharistic prayer (the part of the liturgy that extends from the preface to the Communion-rite, called "Canon of the Mass" in the West). Both sides agree that our Lord becomes truly present on the altar and that His very body and blood are received in Communion. Is it so important salvifically to pinpoint the exact moment of the miracle?

LEAVENED AND UNLEAVENED BREAD

Azyme Controversy

In the Byzantine rite and in most of the Eastern rites, leavened bread (bread made with yeast) is used as the matter for the Holy Eucharist. In the Roman rite and in some Eastern rites, unleavened bread (called "azyme") is used. This discrepancy in usage has been the occasion of extensive polemics between East and West down through the ages.

The apostles most probably used either leavened or azyme bread — whichever was at hand. Our Lord probably used azyme bread at the Last Supper. On the other hand, when our Lord promised the Holy Eucharist at Capharnaum and spoke of himself as the "bread of life" and the "bread that came down from heaven" (John 6), he used the ordinary word for bread which did not indicate any restriction to azyme.

At the reunion Council of Florence, agreement was reached almost without discussion that wheaten bread, whether fermented or not, was the valid matter for the Eucharist. This truth is also stated in the Code of Canon Law, but with the command that all priests make use only of the kind of bread prescribed by their rite. Today the priests of the Latin rites, together with the Armenians, the Malabarese and the Maronites, use unleavened bread, while all the priests of the Byzantine rite together with the Chaldeans, the Copts and the Syrians, use leavened bread.

The Byzantine theologians had many controversies with the azyme-using Armenians before they crossed verbal swords with the Latins. These controversies are reported in some detail by Father Hanssens in his *Institutiones Liturgicae* (Rome, 1930-1932).

The chief anti-azyme anti-Latin polemicist was Nicetas Pectoratus who flourished in the 11th century (MG 120). He summed up his arguments under three headings:

1. The root meaning of the Greek word for bread (*artos*).
2. The Eucharist is a living sacrament.
3. Using azymes constitutes imitation of the Jews.

Nicetas says that the word *artos* used in the Gospels comes from the verb *airo*, rise, hence, bread that rose through fermentation should be used.

He is answered by Cardinal Humbert a Silva Candida, who says that *artos* is often used in Sacred Scripture for both types of bread; hence no argument can be drawn from this.

Nicetas claims that the Holy Eucharist, since it is a sacrament of the living, ought not to be confected with dead matter — as is azyme bread; the action of the yeast in making fermented bread and raising the dough most aptly represents the living character of the Blessed Sacrament.

Cardinal Humbert replies that we receive the Blessed Sacrament as a result of the consecration in the Mass, which is a renewal of our Lord's sacrifice on Calvary. But the whole Passion is the world's greatest example of humility, and hence is aptly renewed with humble azyme-bread; fermented bread is puffed up and thus is not apt to portray the humility of the Passion!

Nicetas thinks that using unleavened bread constitutes too close an imitation of the Jews. This argument is, of course, quite valueless in the controversy. It might just as reasonably be objected against the East that their retention of liturgically solemnizing Saturday as well as Sunday and refusing to make Saturday a fast day also smacks strongly of Jewish influence.

In the sixth century the Armenians defended their use of azymes against the Byzantine theologians by claiming that our Lord used azymes at the Last Supper; that the apostles used both kinds of bread; that the great apostolic Church of Rome also used azymes, thus proving that is was an apostolic tradition! The Armenians also remarked that they themselves were tolerant enough to find no fault with the Byzantine use of fermented bread; why could not the same toleration be shown them in return?

Patriarch Anthimos VII in his encyclical of 1895 states that the Roman Church itself used fermented bread until the 11th century. There is historic evidence that both kinds of bread were used in the Western Church in the early centuries, perhaps even up to the 11th century. However, azymes gradually displaced the leavened bread entirely. The fact that the Armenians as far back as the sixth century appeal to the well-known use of azymes by the Roman Church would argue that azymes were the ordinary form in the West from very early times.

Most Orthodox theologians today agree that both kinds of bread are valid. The opinion of Malinovsky against the validity of azymes is unusual.

The best summation of the whole question is to be found in the tolerant remarks of the Byzantine philosopher Theorian (MG 94) who says that since both kinds of bread are valid, arguments about the matter are as sensible as would be a controversy about whether red wine or white wine would be valid in the liturgy. Besides, says he, after the consecration in the Mass neither fermented nor azyme bread exists any more but only the living body of Christ.

Communion of Children

A custom dating back to the early Church is still maintained by many Orthodox, namely, that of giving Holy Communion to babies and young children. Some Catholics, like the Russians, and recently again by the Melchites, also retain this custom, allowing the child to receive Communion as long as he can be carried to church. Then he waits until his first confession to communicate again, that is, after attaining the use of reason.

Some Orthodox do not interrupt the practice of giving Communion to children, but allow it to continue right up to the first confession. Instead of making his first Communion, he is spoken of as making his first "govenie," or first retreat (recollection) before his first Easter Communion.

An argument sometimes popularly used by some Orthodox is the text in John 6, 54: "Unless you eat the flesh of the Son of Man and drink his blood, you shall not have life in you." They say: "Don't deprive the child of supernatural life," thus making the word "life" stand for sanctifying grace.

But if we study the context of the text adduced, we shall see that our Lord here means life in the sense of "everlasting life in heaven": the Eucharist is a pledge of eternal life. The very next verse reads: "He who eats my flesh and drinks my blood has *life everlasting* and I will raise him up on the last day" (John 6:55).

A child retains in his soul the sanctifying grace which he received at Baptism until he commits a serious sin, which is impossible before he reaches the use of reason.

Why was the practice of giving Communion to young children gradually discontinued in the West? Probably because of fear of profanation. Great reverence for the sacred species developed in the West along other lines too; for example, the practice of each communicant taking the consecrated species into his hands — as was certainly done in the early Roman Church — was eventually discontinued.

DIVORCE

Among all the points of sacramental theology disputed between theologians of the Catholic and of the Orthodox Churches, certainly there is none of more practical importance than that of divorce. The Catholic Church, from the days of the apostles down to the present moment, has held to the sacred dictum of our Lord "What God has joined together, let no man put asunder" (Mark 10:9).

Among the Orthodox, however, a gradual toleration of divorce has been growing. The practice was strengthened when the Emperor Justinian inserted into his great Code of Laws in 542 some license for divorce in case of adultery. By the end of the ninth century this usage was already common practice. At the present time the remarriage of divorced people in the Orthodox Churches constitutes a debated practical hindrance to reunion.

Orthodox Teaching

The Orthodox theologians justify their toleration of divorce by citing the words of our Lord in the Gospel of St. Matthew 19:9: "I say to you, that whoever puts away his wife, except for immorality (Orthodox: adultery) and marries another, commits adultery; and he who marries a woman who has been put away commits adultery."

The Orthodox and many Protestants claim that these words justify divorce because of adultery. They also claim that although a valid marriage endures until the death of one of the parties, there are certain circumstances that can arise when a condition tantamount to death exists between a husband and wife and therefore this "moral" (we would say today "psychic") death dissolves the bond just as certainly as does physical death. Such conditions, for example, would be: serious disease contracted by one of the parties, an absence by one party of five years (and sometimes three years), the crime of one party bringing infamy, the exile of one as a punishment (for example, to Siberia), or any other special case to be judged by the patriarch on its individual merits.

It is interesting to note that although practice in the East was rather lax, it was sometimes reprobated by Church authorities, and Greek theologians admitted on occasion that the practice was an abuse. The great Russian canonist, N. Souvorov, in his *Manual of Church Law* (St. Petersburgh, 1912) says that the Orthodox practice is not that of early tradition when he writes: "The Roman Catholic Church has held firmly to the severe rule of the *discipline of the early ages:* conjugal union is broken only by the death of one of the parties."

Since, however, the text cited above from St. Matthew does pose a problem for explanation, it will be useful to study it and see why tradition and the usual Catholic interpretation do not admit that it endorses divorce.

The first law of Scriptural interpretation demands that we put together all the related texts; truth cannot contradict itself. We must also study the text in the light of its context.

In the 19th chapter of St. Matthew's Gospel we find the Pharisees asking our Lord whether it was lawful to put away one's wife for any motive at all. Both of the great rabbinical schools of our Lord's time held that divorce was licit for the Jews, but they disagreed on the reasons necessary. The school of Shammai held that only adultery was just cause, while the school of Hillel taught that any physical or moral defect in one's wife was cause enough.

Our Lord does not here settle their argument, but proceeds merely to show that any divorce is contrary to primitive revelation by appealing to the witness of the first chapters of Genesis: "Have you not read that the Creator, from the beginning, made them male and female, and said, 'For this cause a man shall leave his father and mother, and cleave to his wife, and the two shall become one flesh?' Therefore, now they are no longer two, but one flesh. What therefore God has joined together, let no man put asunder" (Matt. 19:5-6).

The Pharisees could not deny this clear determination of God's original will, and indeed they taught that marriage was indissoluble for all men except the Jews, for whom there was a privilege. Since our Lord's answer made no mention of their "privilege," they asked why Moses had allowed divorce. Christ answers that it was a concession Moses granted because of the hardness of their hearts, that is, because of their resistance to God's will. But He makes it clear that this was not God's original plan when He instituted marriage. Then He goes on to say: "Amen I say to you, that whoever puts away his wife, except for *immorality*, and marries another, commits adultery; and he who marries a woman who has been put away commits adultery."

Some Protestants and the Orthodox say that Christ here allows divorce for adultery. But to admit this is to accuse our Lord of contradicting himself, for He has just declared that God from the beginning made marriage indissoluble and intended that to remain the pattern. Moreover, in citing the teaching of our Lord on this point, neither St. Mark 10:11-12 nor St. Luke 16:18, make mention of the exception-phrase. And St. Paul, in his first Epistle to the Corinthians 7:10-11, says he is reporting what the Lord himself teaches, namely, that if spouses separate, there is to be no marriage.

Catholic Teaching

What then is the meaning of the phrase in St. Matthew "except for *immorality?*" Catholic exegetes traditionally taught that the phrase "except for immorality" referred to the first part of the statement, namely, it gave the reason for the *separation* of the spouses, but did not give a reason for remarriage. The parallel texts of Sacred Scripture, and the inability of our Lord, Eternal Truth, to contradict himself, justified this interpretation.

However, within the past hundred years, the great progress made in scientific Scripture studies, especially in the field of linguistics, has thrown a completely new light on this text. The Greek word used for "immorality" is *porneia.* Father J. Bonsirven, S. J., a scholar of rabbinical literature, has shown in his work *Le Divorce dans le Nouveau Testament* (Paris, 1948) that *porneia* really means concubinage, or a marriage that was invalid according to Jewish laws. Hence, our Lord would be saying "Whoever puts away his wife (except in the case of a spurious marriage) and marries another . . . "

In his first Epistle to the Corinthians 5:1, St. Paul speaks of the man who married his stepmother, a marriage reprobated by God in Leviticus 18:8, and therefore considered illicit and invalid by the Jews. The word St. Paul uses here to refer to the spurious marriage is *porneia.*

In the Acts of the Apostles we read that the gentile Christians were asked to observe only a few ritual points of the Jewish Law, so that the hoped-for fusion of both elements in the new Christian communities might not be impeded. The Gentiles were asked to abstain from idol-offerings, from blood, from the meat of strangled animals, and from *porneia.* By ordinary Christian morality they were forbidden to indulge in sins of the flesh: why then speak here of *porneia* — unless that term means marriage within the degrees forbidden by God to the Jews?

In the Epistle to the Hebrews 12:16 Esau is called immoral (*pornos*) even though in Genesis we find no mention made of his being guilty of any sexual sins, though we do read that he married Hethite women. Such a marriage outside of Jewry was considered illicit and invalid by the Jews.

In the light, therefore, of these Scriptural arguments and the rabbinical restriction of the term "zenuth" (*porneia*) to designate spurious marriage, the text in St. Matthew becomes considerably clearer.

It is maintained by Monsignor Pospishil in his book *Divorce and Remarriage* (Herder and Herder, New York, 1967), that there is considerable testimony from the early Church Fathers and authorities that the exception phrase in Matt. 19:9, ("whoever puts away his wife, except for immorality") does concede the freedom, to an injured husband, to marry again.

Pospishil says that absolute prohibition of divorce and remarriage appears as common teaching in the West only after the first millenium, whereas a benevolent attitude toward the lesser Christian ideal retained its vigor in the East.

Among the Fathers of the Church, St. Basil († 379) says several times in his Canons (PG. 32, 675 ff.) that an injured husband can be forgiven if he remarries. The "injury" here sustained is either that of the wife's adultery or that of his being abandoned by her.

St. Epiphanius († 403) says the Church tolerates, because of his weakness, the man who takes a second wife after he has separated from the first one who committed adultery (PG. 41, 1024).

St. Cyril of Alexandira († 431) says that adultery destroys the marriage bond completely. He declares that he firmly believes that God has adapted his laws to the measure of human nature (PG. 74, 874).

St. Theodore of Canterbury († 690) says that the husband injured by his wife's adultery may divorce her and marry again. He also says that if a spouse wishes to enter the religious life, the one remaining in the world can marry again (PL 59, 267).

St. Bede the Venerable († c 735) also mentions the same two causes of a marriage's dissolution, namely adultery and entrance into the religious life (PL 92, 85).

St. Boniface of Mainz († 755) teaches the same doctrine; adultery and religious profession dissolve the marriage bond (PL 89, 823).

There are several letters of early popes (e.g. St. Zachary † 752) and canons of early provincial councils (e.g. Milevis, 416) that do not expressly approve remarriage of an injured husband, but imply that such a custom existed at the time.

From the historic evidence adduced from the early Church, it is clear that the Eastern Orthodox Church is really continuing to follow the spirit of "symperiphorá" (consideration) for human "sklerokardía" (hardness of heart), even though their modern practice has gone beyond the usage of the early Church.

Orthodox modern practice in abolishing the double standard and in allowing adulterers to marry again appears in Russian law in 1841 as seen in the "Statutes for Ecclesiastical Consistories" (*Ustav Duchevnych Kensisterij*, St. Petersburgh, 1841), article 256.

In 1905 the Orthodox patriarchs of Constantinople, Alexandria, Antioch and Jerusalem, along with the Metropolitans of Greece, Serbia and Rumania agreed with this ruling. (Zuzek, Ivan, *Kormcaja Kniga*, Rome, 1964).

Adulterers were permitted to remarry, though seven years of penance (usually exclusion from the Eucharist) were prescribed. However, the bishop could shorten this penance.

CHAPTER 7

THE IMMACULATE CONCEPTION AND THE ASSUMPTION

When we speak of the Immaculate Conception of the Blessed Virgin Mary, we are referring to the belief of the Catholic Church that the Blessed Virgin Mary, in the very first instant of her existence in the womb of St. Anne, was preserved free from any least stain of original sin. This privilege was accorded her by God in view of the merits of her future son, the divine Redeemer of the human race.

Mary in the Old Testament

There are several texts of Sacred Scripture that imply the Immaculate Conception. The first of these is the so-called protoevangelium, (Genesis 3:15) where God rebukes and punishes the serpent-devil for seducing our first parents. God says: "I will put enmity between you and the woman, between your seed and her seed; he shall crush your head."

Ancient tradition clearly understood this passage to refer to the Blessed Virgin Mary; that is why the oldest Latin versions of the Bible use the word "she" in the text, "She shall crush thy head." The Hebrew says, "He (or 'it'), namely, the seed shall crush thy head."

A distinguished Father of the early Church, St. Irenaeus († 202) tells us that this passage of Genesis refers to the Blessed Mother. The devil's seed is sin; the Blessed Mother's seed is our Savior, Jesus Christ. God's words set up a parallel between the enmity of Christ and sin and the enmity of the devil and our Lady. The enmity of Christ and sin is absolute and eternal. So, too, should be the enmity between the devil and our Lady. But such an absolute enmity could exist only if the Blessed Mother had never been even for an instant under the devil's power — as she would have been had she come into existence with the taint of original sin on her soul.

Mary in the New Testament

A New Testament text implying the Immaculate Conception is the greeting of the Angel Gabriel to our Lady on the day of her Annunciation. The Angel exclaims: "Hail! Full of grace!" The inspired Greek words of St. Luke's Gospel 1:28 are: *chaire, kecharitomene.* It is remarkable that the Greek used the perfect participle here. The perfect does not refer so much to time or tense in this case, but rather to the kind of action, namely, perfected, fully completed. If the author had wished merely to indicate past time, he had the aorist participles at his disposal. And so the word *kecharitomene* does not mean here simply "having been graced," but rather, "completely graced, perfectly graced."

This same feature of the perfect form in Greek syntax applies also to the imperative and the infinitive. It is, therefore, not just some rare phenomenon we have adduced to prove the point here in question; it is a regular feature of Greek syntax.

Mary in Tradition

The strongest arguments for the Immaculate Conception of the Blessed Virgin, however, are the arguments of tradition. St. Irenaeus, St. Jerome, St. Augustine, St. Ephrem, St. Andrew of Crete, St. Tarasios of Constantiniple — these early saints all teach Mary's Immaculate Conception. The patriarch Photius himself preached eloquently on the Immaculate Conception of our Lady.

The correct doctrine became obscured in the Western Church from the 12th to the 14th century; even St. Thomas Aquinas seems to have been in error on this point. Yet it is most remarkable that the two outstanding Thomists among the Greeks, namely Demetrios Kydonios and Georgios Scholarios, who translated St. Thomas into Greek and were his devoted disciples, did not agree with him on one point only, and that was his failure to admit proof of the Immaculate Conception of our Lady.

Immaculate Conception and Orthodox Belief

In the Greek Church, belief in the Immaculate Conception continued generally until the 15th century, when Nikephoros Xanthopoulos, in his "Commentary on the Feastdays," advanced the idea that our Lady was made immaculate on the feast of the Annunciation. Among the Eastern Slavs, belief in the Immaculate Conception went undisturbed for another 200 years beyond the first Greek doubts, for it was only in the 17th century that John Nathaniel, in his *Skrizhal* (Book of Laws) also put forward Xanthopoulos' views.

What were the reactions of the Greek and Slav Churches to this innovation? Here and there among the Greeks, other theologians adopted Xanthopoulos' view, but many did not, and there are testimonials to general Greek belief in the Immaculate

Conception right up to the 19th century.

After the Pope defined the dogma in 1854, the majority of Greek authors began to oppose it. It is worthy of note that when the Patriarch Anthimos VII wrote his reply to Pope Leo XIII's letter in 1895, and catalogued the "errors" of the Latins, he did not find fault with the West's *belief* in the Immaculate Conception, but objected to the fact that the Pope had *defined* the doctrine.

When Nathaniel's *Skrizhal* appeared in Russia there was a loud outcry against his views on the Immaculate Conception. Especially incensed were the Staroviery or "old-believers" who were devoted to the maintenance of all ancient customs and beliefs, no matter how small or seemingly inconsequential. Accordingly, their opposition to Nathaniel is of special value because of their anger at his violation of *ancient* tradition.

What arguments did the Orthodox theologians adduce for their idea about our Lady being purified on the feast of the Annunciation? They adduce chiefly two patristic citations. One is an expression of St. Gregory Nazianzen (PG 36, 326; PG 36, 634) that our Lord "took human nature, except sin, from the Blessed Virgin Mary, who was *prepurged* in body and soul by the Holy Spirit." This expression of St. Gregory's can be given a completely Catholic interpretation: on the Feast of the Annunciation our Lord became incarnate in the Blessed Virgin whom He had prepurged or sanctified ahead of time in preparation for the event by bestowing upon her the gift of the Immaculate Conception.

St. Gregory is not specifying how far ahead of the event of the Incarnation the "prepurging" of Mary took place. Since the expression can have a perfectly traditional interpretation, why presuppose that St. Gregory disagrees with the other voices of tradition?

The other patristic citation is an expression of St. John Damascene. Referring to the Annunciation, St. John says (PG 94, 835; PG 96, 704) that "the Holy Spirit came upon our Lady and *cleansed* and sanctified her." But if we study the text closely, we shall see that the verb St. John used here is *kathagnizo;* the lexica give the first meaning as cleanse, and the second meaning as hallow, dedicate. In fact, the root word *agnos* means first of all hallowed, sacred to the gods, holy; and only secondarily clean and pure.

The question to settle then is this: which meaning is that of St. John Damascene? We answer confidently that St. John means to say "the Holy Spirit came upon our Lady and *hallowed* and sanctified her." Why? It is idle to say this translation is repetitious or tautological. It is a frequent feature of Greek style to say a thing with two verbs, or three adjectives, or several adverbs — as so many pages of ecclesiastical Greek amply demonstrate. This serves merely to strengthen or to emphasize the expression.

Moreover, in interpreting the Fathers, we ought to apply the same norm that we apply in Sacred Scripture when we say "Sacred Scripture is the best interpreter of Sacred Scripture." In other words, Scripture does not contradict itself. So, too, we must presume that St. John Damascene does not wish to contradict himself in his various works. Yet, in the same homily from which the controverted text is quoted, we find the Saint saying (PG 96, 676) that "God made Mary the image of all holiness in which He could take delight, because this soul was *always directed* only to God and *always turned away* from sin and from sin's parent (the devil)." What does this mean if it does not mean that Mary's soul was preserved free always from every sin?

A further question might be asked here: Does St.

John Damascene ever use the verb *kathagnizo* in other instances and mean by it "to sanctify?" Yes, in a hymn that he composed in honor of our Lady, he uses this verb (PG 96, 852) clearly in the sense of sanctify.

One Orthodox writer, Alexander Lebedev (1903) claims that the Blessed Mother attained her final and complete purgation only under the cross on Good Friday.

In the meantime, the Byzantine Church in all its various usages goes on repeating the glorious trio of adjectives that recur constantly in practically every liturgical service: *panagia* (all-holy one), *achraantos* (the one without even the slightest stain), *hypereulogoumene* (the one blessed beyond all others). Surely this traditional and Catholic faith is the one which even now persists among the vast majority of the Orthodox faithful as they raise their voices from end to end of the Byzantine world and salute our Lady.

Some Orthodox churchmen denied their Church's traditional belief in the bodily Assumption of the Blessed Virgin after Pope Pius XII defined it as a dogma of faith on November 1, 1952. Yet since early Christian times, the East has believed in and celebrated the Assumption of the Blessed Mother, honoring it with a great festival in August which was usually preceded by a fast. In addition, beautiful hymns were composed and sung for this feast.

Among the Slavs the most famous such liturgical reference to the Assumption is found in the *Akafist of the Assumption* printed in Kiev in 1625, and spread from the Ukraine into all of Russia, in which the words occur:

> Blessed are thou, because thy most pure body has been glorified together with thy soul; because the Creator has admitted thee, *Body and Soul*, into Paradise!

Moreover, the majority of all the great churches and monasteries of Russia and of the Ukraine are dedicated to the Blessed Mother, and the majority of these Marian shrines are named in honor of the Assumption.

The question of Our Lady's Assumption — or bodily reception up into heaven — is tied in theologically with the controversy about whether our Lady actually died. Why is the question raised? Because if our Lady was conceived without original sin, then she was never subject to original sin's punishment of death. The objection to this is then made that since our Lord died, our Lady would "appropriately" die too.

The East is not too preoccupied with these questions, referring to the Assumption by the term *Kimisis* (koimesis) or *Uspienie* (falling-asleep). And when Pope Pius XII defined the Assumption of Our Lady as a dogma, he did not settle the death-question, but merely stated that when our Lady's time on earth was finished, she was taken up into heaven body and soul.

CHAPTER 8

THE
CHURCH

Theological Concepts of the Church

Catholic theologians define the Church in the following manner:

> The Catholic Church is the body of true believers in Christ which was instituted by our Lord; these believers form a society whose purpose is eternal salvation; they are united by profession of the same faith, by use of the same sacraments and under the rule of their legitimate pastors, especially the Supreme Pontiff.

All the phrases of that definition are important. The Church is called a body of believers to emphasize the fact that the Church is a visible organization. Today the Jehovah Witnesses strenuously deny this fact as John Calvin and his followers denied it four centuries ago. Calvin claimed that the Church was made up of those souls predestined by God for heaven; only God knew, therefore, who belonged to His Church.

These people seem to forget our Lord's parable about the grain of mustard seed that is an image of the Church in (Matt. 13:31): it is indeed a tiny seed, but when it grows up it reaches the proportions of a tree in whose branches the "birds of the air," i.e., birds from all sides, take up their dwelling. (In Palestine and other Mediterranean countries, the mustard plant grows to the height of a tree; it is not the mere weed known to farmers of our country.)

So, too, the Church of God, from its small beginnings in Palestine 19 centuries ago, would grow and expand until it reached the proportions of a universal haven for souls — its members coming from the "four corners of the earth." This image is surely that of a visible organization.

Moreover, when our Lord commissioned the apostles to go into the whole world teaching and baptizing all nations, He also said that the new converts were to be taught to observe all that He had commanded (Matt. 28:20). But Christ commanded the faithful to obey the apostles as they obey Him: "He who hears you hears Me." And St. Paul exhorted the Church leaders of the Province of Asia, telling them that the Holy Spirit had placed them in positions "to rule the Church of God" (Acts 20:28). Human beings do not rule over invisible organizations. Nor does one rule over human beings that are not organized into a group or society with laws to bind them together.

Catholics also stress the fact that the Church must be the one founded by our Lord. When a Church comes into existence only in the fifth century, like the Nestorians or Monophysites, or in the 16th century, like the Lutherans or Calvinists, or in the 19th century, like the Christian Scientists, it cannot claim very believably to be the Church of Christ.

(Of course the teachers in these bodies will claim

that their body is simply the purified and reformed continuation of the Christian Church that dates back to the days of Christ.)

Members of the true Church should profess the same faith. It is futile to say that those who believe, for example, that Christ is God can be members of the same society as those who say that He was not God, but only a great man. True members of the Church should also make use of the same seven sacraments instituted by Christ. But some people calling themselves Christians believe there are only two sacraments, others one; others deny that there are any.

Most Eastern Orthodox Christians would agree with the full Catholic definition of the Church, given at the beginning of this chapter, until they reach the last phrase — under the rule of the Supreme Pontiff. They substitute phrases like "under the rule of the Holy Spirit," or "of the bishops," or "of Christ and the bishops."

Slavophile Concept of the Church

Traditionally, the Orthodox have held the Catholic definition minus the pope. But in the last century a whole group of theologians and philosophers among the Russians, called the "Slavophiles," have begun to expound new theories about the Church. What their teaching amounts to is this: they lean to the concept of an invisible Church and a Church devoid of any external organization. It almost seems as if the Slavophile doctrine was devised to explain away so much lack of organization in the Orthodox Churches today.

Constantly recurring phrases are such as these: in Christ's Church there is nothing juridical, nothing organizational; the Church is an internal union of love and grace; liberty and harmony join the true believers, etc.

Alexius Khomiakoff (1860) is one of the banner-bearers of Slavophilism. He was a devout layman and a philosopher. He and the other Slavophiles, like Karsavin, Lebedev, Berdiajec, and Kirievsky, all glorify the Russian Orthodox Church above all others. Vladimir Soloviev, a Russian philosopher who became a Catholic, points out the fact that the doctrine of the Slavophiles is based on German and French subjective philosophy and really has nothing truly Slav about it.

Khomiakoff nowhere gives a definition of the Church, but his admirers, Karsavin and Berdiajev, formed one from their master's works. It is: The Church is an intimate and spontaneous synthesis of unity and liberty in love. "Intimate" means the Church is internal and invisible and "spontaneous" means there is nothing juridical about it.

The impression one gets from reading any of these poetical but logically confused phrases is this: These philosophers have set about dreaming up a scheme for a Church which would suit their own fancies, instead of starting out — as true theologians and scientific investigators must — with the question, "What did our Lord say about His Church?"

The Slavophiles lamentably fail to start out by investigating all our Lord's statements and parables about the kingdom of God and the kingdom of heaven, as well as the other inspired records of the visible and organized Church, found delineated in the Acts of the Apostles and especially in the Epistles of St. Paul.

There are some favorite words that the Slavophiles bandy about; one of these is "Juridicism." They claim that the Catholic Church is guilty of three forms of Juridicism:

1. *Secularism*, by which Church government is "reduced" to the same modes as civil government.

2. *Exaggeration*, by which law is made the whole basis of unity.
3. *Arbitrariness*, by which the powers and rights of the individual bishops are limited by the pope.

In answer to this, Catholics point to the regrettable condition of the Orthodox Churches as schisms multiply and no central authority is at hand to curb vagaries of doctrine and abuses of practice among them. Somewhat grudgingly the Orthodox admit that the Catholics have perfect organization, but they decry it.

Lebedev, in his book *On the Supremacy of the Pope* (1903, St. Petersburg) says:

The Latin Church has indeed a very strong and perfect organization. It is built like a pyramid. It is an absolute and monolithic monarchy. But is this absolute unity proper to the Church of Christ? Unhesitatingly we reply: not at all, not at all!

Sobornost

Slavophiles believe that all the life and qualities of the Church are communicated to each individual member, including infallibility. This possession of everything by everybody they call "Sobornost." Hence, they say the word *katholikos* in Greek is to be derived not from *kath'holen* (meaning "over the whole earth") as Catholics say, but from *kath'holon* (meaning "according to each individual member").

Khomiakoff says that the Eastern Orthodox Church lives a "life of love" built on grace and "Sobornost," while all the Western Christians lead a "life of rationalism" — the Protestants by relying on their own private judgment and the Catholics by relying on the judgment of the pope. He also says that the internal life of the Church (grace) is opposed to the external (juridical) life. Catholics hold that both are necessary and complement one another.

The Slavophiles, by their insistence upon "Sobornost" and the importance of each individual member of the Church, seem to destroy the concept of the hierarchy. Soloviev says the Slavophiles want a perfect Church, but by undermining the pope's supremacy they deprive the Church of the means to attain it — namely, a head and government for the body.

Father George Florovsky, a prominent modern Orthodox theologian, wrote a book called *The Church of God* (London, 1934). He stresses the concept of the Church as the Mystical Body of Christ and denies Soloviev's charge. He states that in the Mystical Body each member has his part to play and the bishops have their part as well. But Catholics reply that by admitting "Sobornost," the Orthodox destroy the practical importance and authority of the hierarchy.

Orthodox theologians of this century are very much concerned with the doctrine of the Mystical Body. Akvilonov says that the doctrine of the Church of Christ is fully contained in the single concept of the Mystical Body of Christ. Lebedev claimed that forgetfulness of this doctrine of the Mystical Body caused the Latins to overlook the truth that Christ is the head of the Church. But Lebedev is wrong on his facts. St. Thomas and St. Bonaventure treat this doctrine, too, as did St. Augustine. And it was discussed at the Council of Florence in 1438.

It is true that Latin manuals of theology did not devote much space to it. But that was because the West had to battle the tenets of Protestants regarding the invisible nature of the Church. In modern times, because of the stress of social consciousness, the truths about the Mystical Body are more thoroughly treated by Catholic authors, and one of the finest treatments of the doctrine is Pope Pius XII's encyclical "Mystici Corporis." Moreover, the Orthodox seem to ignore the Catholic distinction between Christ as the invisible Head of the Church and the pope, His Vicar on earth, as the visible head of the Church.

Orthodox insistence on the invisible nature of the Church fits in with the traditional Eastern idea of passivity — leaving things largely up to God. Thus, if there are errors or abuses or problems in the Church, the Holy Spirit will inspire the remedy for them. If God wants new believers added to His Church, He will accomplish this without the activity and labors of missionaries. If one monk leads a perfect life in the monastery as a contemplative, he gives more glory to God than any number of active but imperfect missionaries, etc.

But the East should not overlook the fact that Christ, as the all-knowing God, foresaw the difficulties His followers would encounter if they did not have a visible head, and hence, gave them a head in St. Peter and his successors.

Moreover, in defending the passivity of the East, some lose sight of the fact that Christ commissioned the apostles to go into the whole world and preach the Gospel to every creature. And He surely meant those words not only for the 12 apostles personally but for their successors as well, because He added the words: "And behold I am with you all days, even to the consummation of the world." But the apostles were not going to live until the end of the world; the Lord expressly foretold persecution and death for them.

The basic defect in all this Slavophile thinking seems to be the denial of true secondary causality. Our Lord's death, for example, won salvation for all men, together with merits and graces sufficient to save many worlds besides our own. And yet, He tells His followers that they must suffer, too, for their salvation: "If anyone wishes to come after me, let him deny himself, and take up his cross daily, and follow me" (Luke 9:23). And St. Paul sums up the mystery in that classic phrase in the Epistle to the Philippians: "Work out your salvation with fear and trembling" (Phil. 2:12).

In recent years Orthodox leaders have achieved considerable abandonment of passivity. This is evidenced by a widespread effort to improve the education of candidates for the priesthood, by zealous attempts at long last to give religious instruction to the young, by undertaking some missionary apostolate in unevangelized countries, and in trying to solve embarrassing overlappings of ecclesiastical jurisdiction.

CHAPTER 9

THE PRIMACY OF THE POPE

Our Lord instituted His Church as a visible society. He compared it to a small mustard seed planted in the earth which grew up to become a plant, a bush and finally a tree (Matthew 13:31), so that the birds could come from all sides and dwell in its branches. He founded it as a society of men united for a single purpose: the salvation of their souls.

To fulfill this purpose they need laws. Christ gave His laws into the keeping of His apostles: "Go, therefore, and make disciples of all nations, baptizing them in the name of the Father, and of the Son, and of the Holy Spirit, teaching them to observe all that I have commanded you" (Matthew 28:19f.).

But no visible society of men could remain united in belief and effort and purpose without any leaders. And so Christ made the apostles the Church's first bishops. But even the bishops cannot remain united without a head, a thing which is true of any society. And so Christ made St. Peter the head of the bishops and thus supreme pastor of His Church. But His Church was to endure until the end of the world: "Behold, I am with you all days, even unto the consummation of the world" (Matthew 28:20). Hence, the successors of St. Peter, the bishops of Rome, are the heads of the Church of Christ until the end of time.

When we study the evidence to establish the fact that the bishop of Rome, the pope, is the head of Christ's Church, we must proceed by three logical steps. We must show that:

1. Christ made St. Peter the head of the Church.

2. St. Peter acted as pope and died at Rome.

3. The early popes really considered themselves heads of the whole Church; they acted accordingly, and their rule was accepted.

The "Petrine" Texts

Let us first consider how Christ made St. Peter the head of His Church. Our Lord's intention in this respect is made abundantly clear by a study of the three passages of the Gospel called the "Petrine texts." All through the Gospels we find Peter taking the initiative and speaking for the other apostles. So it is also on that momentous occasion when our Lord declared that St. Peter was going to be the head of His Church.

> Now Jesus having come into the district of Caesarea Philippi, began to ask his disciples, saying, 'Who do men say the Son of Man is?' But they said, 'Some say, John the Baptist; and others, Elias; and others, Jeremias, or one of the prophets.' He said to them, 'But who do you say that I am?' Simon Peter answered and said, 'Thou art the Christ, the Son of the living God.' Then Jesus answered and said, 'Blessed art thou, Simon Bar-Jona, for flesh

and blood has not revealed this to thee, but my Father in heaven. And I say to thee, thou art Peter (Rock) and upon this rock I will build my Church, and the gates of hell shall not prevail against it. And I will give thee the keys of the kingdom of heaven; and whatever thou shalt bind on earth shall be bound in heaven, and whatever thou shalt loose on earth shall be loosed in heaven' (Matthew 16:13-19).

In this text our Lord shows that He was going to make St. Peter the head of the Church by using three different figures of speech: He calls Peter the "Rock" on which the Church would be built; He says that Peter holds the keys of the kingdom of heaven; He uses the Hebrew image of binding and loosing which indicates the power to impose an obligation or to free from it: hence, the power to rule. The promise that the gates of hell would never prevail against the "Rock" is a promise of something that would last forever, namely, even after Peter's death. Therefore, it was something given to Peter's position and would continue on in his successors.

The obvious sense of this text is so clear for the primacy that some Protestant theologians try to deny the authenticity of the text. But that is a vain resort; this text is as authentic as any in the Gospels. Great Lutheran authorities like Dr. Heinrich Holtzmann of the University of Strasbourg admit that if the text is genuine it certainly means that St. Peter is made head of the Church.

Luther said the words "on this rock I will build my Church" mean "on faith like yours I will build my Church." But he completely overlooks two arguments against such an interpretation. First, there is a play on the words *Peter* and *rock*. In Aramaic *Kepha* was St. Peter's name given by our Lord himself (John 1:42); hence, what our Lord said was: "Thou art the Rock and on this rock I shall build my Church." Moreover our Lord goes on to apply to Peter personally the other metaphors: "I will give to *thee* the keys of the kingdom of heaven, and whatsoever *thou* shalt bind on earth, etc."

Orthodox theologians give Luther's meaning to the words, but with no more convincing results. Certain great Eastern doctors said that the words apply to the person of St. Peter who is made by Christ the head of His Church.

St. Cyril of Alexandria († 444), in his commentary on St. Matthew's Gospel, says that by the words "on this rock I shall build my Church," Christ makes Peter its pastor: literally *he places Peter over it* as shepherd.

(ταύτης ποιμένα τὸν Πέτρον ἐφίστησιν) (PG 72, 423).

St. Gregory of Nyssa († 395), in a sermon on St. Stephen, speaks of St. Peter as head of the Church in these terms: "According to the privilege granted him by the Lord, he (Peter) is *that unbreakable and most solid rock upon which the Savior built His Church.*"

(ἡ ἀρραγὴς καὶ ὀχυρωτάτη πέτρα, ἐφ᾽ ἣν τὴν Ἐκκλησίαν ὁ Σωτὴρ ᾠκοδόμησε) (PG 46 733).

Our Lord clearly foresaw and foretold the fact that Peter would deny Him. But that was only a temporary lapse; it would not impair his efficacy to rule the Church later on. Christ says this clearly in St. Luke's Gospel:

And the Lord said, Simon, Simon, behold, Satan has desired to have you, (i.e., *you* plural, referring to all the apostles) that he may sift you as wheat. But I have prayed *for thee*, that *thy faith* may not fail (prayer for the individual, St. Peter); and do thou, when once thou hast turned again, strengthen thy brethren (Luke 22:31-32).

The fact that Christ not only promised but after His Resurrection actually conferred the primacy on St. Peter is evident from St. John's Gospel:

> When, therefore, they had breakfasted, Jesus said to Simon Peter, 'Simon, son of John, dost thou love me more than these do?' He said to him, 'Yes, Lord, thou knowest that I love thee.' He said to him, 'Feed my lambs.' He said to him a second time, 'Simon, son of John, dost thou love me?' He said to him, 'Yes, Lord, thou knowest that I love thee.' He said to him, 'Feed my lambs.' A third time he said to him, 'Simon, son of John, dost thou love me?' Peter was grieved because he said to him for the third time 'Dost thou love me?' And he said to him, 'Lord, thou knowest all things, thou knowest that I love thee.' He said to him, 'Feed my sheep' (John 21:15-17).

The Greek text is very graphic. Instead of "feed my sheep" — a justified but inadequate rendering — it should read *"shepherd my flocks."* The word *probatia* is wider than just sheep — it means *flocks* of any kind. And the verb *poimaine* from poimaino, derived from poimen, a shepherd, portrays the same picture-action as our English verb *to shepherd* from the noun shepherd.

This triple declaration of love by St. Peter was a magnificent reparation for his threefold denial of his Master and the Master rewarded it by making Peter the supreme shepherd in His place. Our Lord has already called His followers His sheep and referred to himself as the Good Shepherd over the whole flock, both the lambs and the sheep.

Orthodox authors say that our Lord is simply reinstating St. Peter as an apostle in good standing after the triple denial. Yet, listen to what an Orthodox theologian says about such a dodge: "The words of Christ, 'feed my lambs, feed my sheep' contain the whole doctrine of the papacy . . . which follows certainly as a corollary from them. Our theologians don't know how to explain them, except to keep repeating like parrots: 'All the apostles are equal; no one is greater than others.' That is why the bishop of Rome is equal only to the bishop of Kaluga (a little suburban town near Moscow). How such arguments are repugnant to our Russian honesty!" (Vassili Rosanov, *Along the Walls of the Church*, St. Petersburg, 1906).

St. John Chrysostom († 407) says in several places that St. Peter's threefold denial of Christ was so atoned for by his triple confession of love that he was not only reinstated in his apostolic office, but was given the supreme position in the Church. After the confession of love, St. John Chrysostom says in his 88th Homily on St. John's Gospel (PG 59, 478) that St. Peter was the "most eminent of the apostles, and the mouthpiece of the disciples, and the leader of their group."

$$(\text{ἔκκριτος ἦν τῶν ἀποστόλων, καὶ στόμα τῶν}$$
$$\mu\alpha\theta\eta\tau\tilde{\omega}\nu, \kappa\alpha\grave{\iota} \kappa\rho\upsilon\phi\grave{\eta} \tau\sigma\tilde{\upsilon} \chi\rho\rho\sigma\tilde{\upsilon})$$

In the fifth homily on Penitence, Chrysostom says that after so great a fault committed by his denial, St. Peter not only was restored to his former honor *but was also given jurisdiction over the universal Church (PG 49, 308).*

$$(\tau\grave{\eta}\nu \text{ ἐπιστασίαν τῆς οἰκουμενικῆς}$$
$$\text{Ἐκκλησίαν ἐνεχείρισε})$$

Again, in his eighth discourse on the Jews, Chrysostom again praises the repentance of St. Peter which so thoroughly wiped out his fault that (PG 48, 951) *he becomes again head of the apostles and the whole world is committed to his care.*

(Ὡς καὶ πρῶτος γενέσθαι τῶν ἀποστόλων καὶ τὴν
οἰκουμένην ἐγχειρισθῆναι ἅπασαν)

From the three Petrine texts in the Gospels we
see the Primacy of Peter clearly taught. St. Peter is
obviously the leader all through the Gospels; St.
Peter's name occurs 60 times; no other apostle's
name appears more than 25 times.

Dr. Francis Dvornik in his "Byzantium and the
Roman Primacy" says that our Petrine texts were
already in common use to prove papal authority by
the end of the second century. If, therefore, they
were "common" around 190, then they were in use
for some time before.

St. Peter, Acting as Head of the Church

After the Ascension of our Lord into heaven we
find St. Peter acting as the head of the Church; he
directs the election of Judas' successor (Acts 1:15);
he preaches the first sermons after the descent of
the Holy Spirit (Acts 2:14; 3:12; 5:29); he judges
Ananias and Sapphira (Acts 5); he leads the gentiles
into the Church (Acts 10:11); he settles the dispute
at the Council of Jerusalem (Acts 15).

When persecution in Palestine scattered the
Christians, St. Peter went to Antioch and then to
Rome. Even though the great bishoprics of the early
Church like Rome, Alexandria, Antioch and Jerusalem jealously preserved the catalogue of their bishops' names (and Antioch, indeed, traced her line of
bishops back to St. Peter) yet we never find anyone
in the early Church contesting the right of the
bishop of Rome to rule in St. Peter's place because
St. Peter died at Rome, in the place where he finally
fixed his See. All ancient tradition says that St.
Peter established his See at Rome and died there.

During a period of 20 years (1940-1960), excavations under the Altar of the Confession in St. Peter's

Basilica have produced archaeological discoveries as evidence that the apostle Peter had been buried there.

A Greek inscription dating to about 160 A.D. states that "Peter is within." From this and other inscriptions it becomes clear that, at least since the middle of the second century, the faithful have been convinced that St. Peter's tomb was in the place marked by the chapel under the present papal altar. Dr. Margherita Guarducci, the distinguished Italian archaeologist and foremost authority on the epigraphy of the excavations, states: " . . . we can now say that in the investigation of St. Peter's tomb, science has come to the aid of faith. This happy alliance has placed on age-old tradition a strengthened and renewed seal of irrefutable Truth" (*Tomb of St. Peter,* New York, 1960).

Dr. Adolf von Harnack, outstanding non-Catholic scholar and student of early Christian literature, says that to deny St. Peter's presence and death in Rome is *"durchaus kindisch"* (downright childish).

Successors of St. Peter

Did St. Peter's successors consider themselves heads of the whole Church in his place? The history and tradition of the early Church point to it. There is extant a letter of Pope St. Clement from about the year 95. It was written to the Corinthians who had rebelled against their clergy. St. Clement not only advises obedience, he *commands* it and reminds the Corinthians that disobedience to his commands will be sinful.

This St. Clement lived and worked with St. Peter and St. Paul; should he not have known the mind of the early Church? And notice, St. Clement, third successor of St. Peter, judges the Corinthians from faraway Rome when St. John, the apostle, was still alive in the nearer city of Ephesus!

A few years later, when St. Ignatius of Antioch was on his way to Rome to suffer martyrdom, he wrote seven letters, one of which he addressed to the Christians in Rome in which he declares that their Church presides over all the others. Non-Catholic historians like Harnack, Loomis, and Shotwell agree that St. Ignatius considered Rome's bishops rulers over the others.

There is extant a letter of Pope St. Telesphorus from the early second century (c. 120). It was written to the bishop of Alexandria (Egypt). The pope says he has heard that the number of converts to Christianity is growing so fast that not all of them — because of crowding — can attend the Sunday liturgy. The pope then tells the bishop to have as many liturgies celebrated on each Sunday as will be necessary to accommodate the Christian community. (Besides being an exemplification of papal primacy, this letter is remarkable for the light it throws on two other disciplines of the early Church: first, that Sunday has definitely displaced Saturday as the day of Christian worship; and secondly, that in those early days only one liturgy was celebrated, the bishop and clergy and people all gathered together for community worship.)

When, toward the end of the second century, Pope St. Victor threatened to excommunicate the bishops of Asia (Province of Asia) because they did not follow the Roman custom of celebrating Easter always on a Sunday, St. Irenaeus of Lyons and other bishops wrote to him to ask him not to do it, saying that such a penalty was very severe. But they did not even think of questioning his authority to do so if he wished.

St. Irenaeus, who died in the year 202, wrote a great book entitled *Against Heresies.* He was a Greek, a disciple of St. Polycarp who had been instructed by St. John the Apostle. In his book, St.

Irenaeus says that the Roman Church is universally known for its foundation and organization by the glorious apostles Peter and Paul. Then he goes on to say that "because of its preeminent authority, every church must agree with this Church."

Outstanding testimonials to the pope's authority appear in the third century in the writings of St. Cyprian. St. Cyprian argued with Popes St. Cornelius and St. Stephen, but he did not deny their authority. In fact he declares the bishops of Rome to be the successors of St. Peter and thus the Roman See is "the mother and root of the Catholic Church." And St. Cyprian, writing from North Africa, urges Pope St. Stephen I to excommunicate the bishop of Arles (in France), saying that he was a Novatian heretic. Obviously, St. Cyprian recognized the pope's wide jurisdiction.

When we reach the fourth century, exemplifications of the pope's use of universal jurisdiction are so numerous that anyone who wishes to read history can see the facts for himself. If these facts are so evident even to non-Catholic historians, why do they not accept the primacy? How do they argue against it? Both the Orthodox and the Protestants say that each of these instances of papal exercise of authority merely goes to show the overweening lust for power on the part of the bishops of Rome and that the papal actions represent a usurpation of authority.

Catholic theologians insist that the arguments for the papal primacy form a cumulative argument; in other words, this great consistency on the part of the popes exercising their universal jurisdiction shows a definite pattern. It is a plan of action flowing from inner conviction. It is exercised by popes who were personally very holy and saintly men (e.g. St. Leo the Great, † 461) and not proud or overbearing autocrats.

If each instance of the exercise of papal jurisdiction were considered by itself, apart from all other instances, it would be possible to say, as do many Orthodox, that some individual instance is an accident of history or a proof of papal interference. But such a contention is impossible if we consider each incident as part of the whole or cumulative argument.

The Orthodox theory also ignores the fact that those over whom the popes exercised their jurisdiction either accepted it as the proper thing or at least did not gainsay it. Moreover, the positive testimonials of great bishops like Ignatius of Antioch, Irenaeus of Lyons and Cyprian of Carthage support the doctrine of the Roman See's primacy quite apart from any particular instance of its use.

The popes exercised their universal jurisdiction because they believed they were the heads of the Church in virtue of being the heirs to St. Peter's primacy. This is the teaching too, of great Eastern Fathers of the Church and is particularly clear in the writings of St. Theodore the Studite († 826), as for example in his letter to Pope Paschal I, (PG 99-1151).

> Hear me, O head of the apostles, placed by God as shepherd (pastor, $\pi o\mu\acute{\eta}\nu$) of the sheep of Christ, holder of the keys of the kingdom of heaven, the rock of faith on which the Catholic Church has been built. For you are Peter; you adorn the throne of Peter and rule from it.
>
> (Πέτρος γὰρ σὺ, τὸν Πέτρου θρόνον κοσμῶν καὶ διέπων)

At the first Ecumenical Council (Nice in 325), the pope, St. Sylvester, and the whole Western or Latin Church was represented by one bishop, one priest and one deacon. This Council established the prestige of the great sees of Christendom as patriarchal. Yet, at the end of the Council, its acts were signed first by the Roman legates even ahead of the Eastern patriarchs, because these legates, even the priest and the deacon, represented the pope. And even though the papal legates signed the decrees, the Emperor Constantine dispatched a special delegation to Rome posthaste in order to get the pope's own signature too.

At the second Ecumenical Council held at Constantinople in 381, some Eastern bishops wanted Constantinople to have the second place of honor among the patriarchs, or chief bishops, right after Rome. Pope St. Damasus protested, saying that that place belonged traditionally to Alexandria.

After the Council of Chalcedon some of the Eastern bishops framed a law, the famous 28th Canon, saying that Constantinople should have equal rights with Rome. Pope St. Leo rejected this Canon and refused to confirm it. It is actually missing from the oldest codices of the acts of the Council, both Latin and Greek.

St. Augustine, bishop of Hippo (North Africa) in the early fifth century, wrote to Rome to settle a dispute with the Pelagian heretics. When the papal answer was received, St. Augustine declared simply and forcefully: "Roma locuta est: causa finita est" (Rome has spoken: the case is finished) (PL 39, 734).

When the famous Photius was seeking the pope's favor and confirmation of his having replaced St. Ignatius as patriarch of Constantinople, he was very cognizant of the pope's primacy, but when he was at odds with Rome, he said that the papal primacy was due to the fact that Rome was formerly the capital of the Empire; now that the capital had shifted to Constantinople, so should the primacy.

In the 11th century, Michael Caerularius, to justify his position of opposition to Rome, said that the pope used to be the head of the Church until he fell into heresy (over the Filioque). Now the primacy has passed to the "New Rome," Constantinople. It is interesting to note that Patriarch Peter of Antioch wrote to Caerularius protesting the break with Rome and reminding him that if any place other than Rome had the right to be the chief see of the Church it was Antioch, because St. Peter had been bishop there before he went to Rome. And yet, Antioch never made any such pretentions because St. Peter died at Rome and so left the primacy there.

During the 15th century, the monk Philaret of Pskov devised the theory that since Constantinople had fallen into the hands of the Turks (1453), the headship of the Church now passed to Moscow which he hailed as the "Third Rome." He claimed that the Greeks fell before the Turkish armies because they entered into union with Old Rome at Florence (1438). He said the true Church of Christ was now to be found only in Russia, and added — quite gratuitously — that Moscow would continue to be the Church's capital until the end of the world!

Two great Russian converts to the Catholic Church, Fathers J. Gagaria and A. Galitzin, draw attention to the fact that the Byzantine liturgy itself makes eloquent reference to the primacy of the pope. Every year on the feast of Pope St. Clement (Nov. 25) the whole Orthodox East joins the Catholic East in singing: "Peter, the Prince of the Apostles, left thee as a worthy successor of himself; after him thou didst rule the Church most capably."

On the feast of Pope St. Martin (Apr. 13), all sing: "O Martin, thou hast adorned the divine See of Peter and by means of his divine rock thou hast preserved the Church unbroken."

On February 18, the feast of Pope St. Leo the Great, all sing: "As the successor of the divine Peter, enriched with his presidency and primacy, Leo published his divinely inspired definition."

The reference here is to St. Leo's long letter to the Council of Chalcedon (451), condemning Monophysitism. When it was read at the Council, the bishops all exclaimed: "Peter speaks through Leo!" The matter was settled in accordance with the pope's definition.

After this Council, the Eastern patriarchs, namely, Maximos of Antioch, Anatolius of Constantinople and Juvenal of Jerusalem composed a letter to Pope St. Leo the Great giving an account of the Council held under the presidency of his legates — a Council that condemned Monophysitism because of the masterly exposition of the true Catholic doctrine contained in Pope Leo's letter to the Council. Among other things the Eastern patriarchs clearly recognized the pope's primacy, saying:

> You have indeed preserved the faith, which has come down to us like a golden stream flowing at the command of our divine teacher. Constituted, as you are, the interpreter of the words of the Blessed Peter for all mankind, you have poured forth upon the universe the blessings he elicited by his faith. Hence we have looked to you as to the leader of our religion to our great advantage. You indeed, as the head among the members, presided here in the person of your representatives, who led the way by their correct counsel.

Later on in the letter, in speaking of the excesses of Patriarch Dioscoros of Alexandria whom the Council deposed and who had planned to excommunicate the pope, they said:

> He extended his fury even against him who had been entrusted by the Savior with the

guardianship of the vineyard — we mean your Holiness — and planned his excommunication, after you have been so zealous to keep the body of the Church united!

You will ask: "What do Orthodox theologians say about this clear testimony of the Church Fathers at Chalcedon?" A group of Orthodox theologians was asked this question recently by a Catholic priest and one replied: "The expressions used by the Fathers at Chalcedon are nothing more than Oriental imagery and flattery."

If such is the case, then how can we ever be sure just when an Eastern Father is stating something dogmatically correct and when he is indulging in "Oriental imagery?" For example, does St. John Chrysostom really think our Lady is holier than the angels or is he merely using Eastern flattery when he sings so beautifully: "Higher in honor than the Cherubim and more glorious beyond compare than the Seraphim, who without harm to thy virginity didst give birth to the Word of God: thee we extol, true Mother of God!"?

(Commemoration of Our Lady after the Consecration in the liturgy of St. John Chrysostom.)

Further Notes on the Primacy

There are several points of interest regarding the primacy that Dr. Hans Küng raised in his book *The Church.* They are found chiefly in the last section of his book, entitled *The Offices of the Church.*

The present author wrote an article for the Vol. 4, No. 3, (1969) edition of *Diakonia*, in which he takes exception to Küng's remarks. With the editor's permission, some of that article is reprinted here.

Küng's book *The Church* has received much praise; but the book does not seem to merit absolute superlatives.

Dr. Küng does not appear to leave room for the

well-known development of dogma in the early Church regarding the primacy when he unduly emphasizes that the evidence is not *abundant* in the first centuries. Actually, it is remarkable that there is *any* evidence at all from the early centuries when one considers that persecution wracked the Christian communities, on and off, from the beginning of Nero's persecution in 64 until Constantine's Edict of Toleration in 313. It is quite remarkable enough that we have even the testimonies that have come down to us, such as the letters of St. Clement (c. 95), and St. Telesphorus (c. 125), or the actions of St. Victor (c. 190), and St. Cornelius (c. 252).

Surely, St. Irenaeus means to do more than cite interesting travelogue material when he says that Christians of his time were proud to know the names of their local bishops back to the first one and the names of the bishops of Rome back to Peter. (St. Irenaeus died a martyr in 202 — after having ruled the See of Lyons for about forty years). [1]

Dr. Küng constantly makes statements alluding to those who call texts into question but without stating the solution to them readily found by Catholic scholars. For example, he says (p. 464): "There is a world of difference in interpretation between interpreting Matt. 16:18 in the light of Matt. 18:18, or vice versa."

True. But since Matt. 16:18 must be looked at in the light too, of Luke 22 and John 21, the answer is that what is given to all the apostles in Matt. 18:18, namely the power to bind and to loose, is given specifically and especially to Peter along with his other prerogatives. The fundamental rule of hermeneutics by which we say that "Scripture best interprets Scripture" must not be abandoned here any more than we should fail to use it elsewhere.

---

[1] Adversus Haereses, III, 3,3; pg. 7,849.

Dr. Küng seems to find arrogance in the statement of Pope Innocent († 407) that important matters discussed by synods of bishops should be submitted to the bishop of Rome for his decision. Why should this be frowned upon? Even at the great ecumenical councils, (for example, the first two, namely Nicaea I in 325 and Constantinople I in 381), the decrees, after being signed by the patriarchs and bishops present, were rushed off to Rome by the emperors (Constantine and Theodosius respectively) to be signed by the pope.[2] Anyhow, Innocent's statement loses all semblance of severity when it declares that Peter, "the heir of this name and honor . . . *can help* all the Churches throughout the world."[3]

Between the first two ecumenical councils, the completely Eastern synod of Sardica took place in 344. This council considered specifically the point of appeal to Rome. It says that every bishop has the right to appeal to the pope — "to the head, that is, to the See of the Apostle Peter."[4] I mention this because Dr. Küng laments the fact that the primacy was not treated explicitly by Fathers united in council. Sardica took care of the question in the

---

[2] It might be well too, to point out that all the testimonies to the fact that the early Church recognized the pope as head of the Church could be explained away if we take each instance *alone*. Pope Victor's stand on the Eastern controversy (end of the third century), for example, could be called unwarranted interference in the affairs of the Church beyond his patriarchate. The same could be said of St. Telesphorus's letter to the bishop of Alexandria directing that multiple liturgies be celebrated on Sunday (early second century).

But it is our contention that these actions by the pope represent a pattern of primacy's use: in other words, they are to be taken cumulatively, not individually.

[3] Ep. XXX, 2 (PL. 20, 590).

[4] Mansi, Sacrorum Conciliorum . . . Collectio, T. VI, col. 1142.

East; Nicaea I named the patriarchs, and the bishop of Rome was named patriarch of the West. The West therefore already looked to the Roman bishop as its natural patriarchal head.

It is clear that the East acted on Sardica's decree without demur, for St. John Chrysostom († 407) — sent into exile by a synod of Constantinople convened by his enemy, the Empress Eudoxia — promptly appealed to the pope, asking him to annul the acts of the synod.[5] And St. Basil the Great († 379) wrote to Pope St. Damasus, begging him to send legates to the East to settle the numerous disputes troubling the Church there.[6]

Father Küng seems to find some diminution of Peter's glory (actually, he seems to find almost a cancellation of it) in the fact that after each honorific primacy test, St. Peter is rebuked by the Lord. For example, when St. Peter demurs at the Lord's prophecy concerning His impending passion in Matt. 16, Jesus says to him: "Get behind me, satan." And after the Lord confers the primacy on Peter in John 21 (Feed my lambs, "shepherd my flock" — as the Greek clearly reads), He also rebuked Peter for wanting to know what will happen to John in the future: "If I wish him to remain until I come, what is it to thee?" A Catholic exegete would not find that these verses cloud the glory of the primacy statements at all. They actually serve to glorify the choice of so weak and human a man as Peter to be the head of the Church: The Church has to be divine to survive in spite of such human weakness.

Father Küng sometimes excuses himself from the burden of demonstrating his statements by saying: "It is impossible here . . . " (e.g. 455, 483). But he finds it possible, time after time, to assert that the primacy must be one, not of glory and titles and

[5] PG. 32 433, Epist. 70.
[6] PG. 52, 529-536.

dominion, but of ministry and of pastoral service. Again, with less repetition of the theme that papalists legalistically founded Petrine dominion on the false decretals, there might have been room, for example, to point out that the popes were *forced* by chaotic political circumstances to assume the civil rule of Rome as the Eastern emperors abandoned the defense of central Italy.

Father Küng seems surprised that St. Ignatius of Antioch (107) in writing his letter to the Romans, does not address an individual monarchical bishop by name (p. 460) although he does this for the communities to whom he writes in Asia Minor. There is a very ready answer for this: St. Ignatius could hardly be sure *who* was bishop in Rome in the early second century.[7] Persecution was rife; all the bishops of Rome from St. Peter in 67 to St. Melchiades in 314 died as martyrs. Some lasted only a short time. For example, St. Anterus, who ruled from November, 235, to January, 236, doubtless ascended the throne and descended it again in violent death without anyone in Syria even hearing that he had been pope — given the communications of those days!

---

[7] Dr. Quasten, in his Patrology, Vol. I, pp. 68-70, says that considerable research has been done on this letter of St. Ignatius, especially by J. Thiele and A. Ehrhard, and he concludes that "it is the earliest avowal of the Primacy of Rome that we possess from the pen of a non-Roman ecclesiastic."

CHAPTER 10

THE
FILIOQUE
CONTROVERSY

Dogmatic Issue of the Doctrine Itself

One of the oldest subjects of controversy between East and West had to do with the procession of the Holy Spirit. It is often called the "Filioque" dispute because of the fact that in the Western Church the word "Filioque" was eventually added to the Nicene Creed. There are really two points at issue in the controversy:

1. The doctrinal truth about the question of the procession of the Holy Spirit.
2. The legitimacy of adding the word "Filioque" to the Creed.

Let us first consider the doctrine involved.

The Orthodox maintain that the Holy Spirit proceeds from the Father alone; the Catholics teach that the Holy Spirit proceeds from the Father and the Son as from one principle.

The Orthodox claim that their doctrine is based on the testimony of Sacred Scripture which explicitly states that the Holy Spirit proceeds from the

Father, but nowhere explicitly states that He proceeds from the Son. The text they adduce is from St. John's Gospel 15:26: "But when the Advocate has come, whom I will send you from the Father, the Spirit of truth who proceeds from the Father, he will bear witness concerning me."

The Catholics say that this text is assertive, but not exclusive, and it must be so because other texts of Sacred Scripture teach implicitly the fact that the Holy Spirit proceeds also from the Son. Hence, Catholics like to quote the brilliant words of St. Anselm, when he says in regard to this controversy: "The words 'the Holy Spirit proceeds from the Son' do not occur in Sacred Scripture; but Sacred Scripture does make assertions by which it may be proved, and it makes no statements by which it may be denied" (PL 158, 321).

Let us examine some of these assertions of Sacred Scripture that teach implicitly the Catholic doctrine. St. Paul says in the Epistle to the Galatians 4:6: " . . . God has sent the *Spirit of his Son* into our hearts . . . " It is a commonplace of Scriptural interpretation that when St. Paul uses the word "God" as subject of an action, he means God the Father. Hence, in this text from Galatians we have the implicit teaching that the Holy Spirit proceeds from the Father and the Son, because the Father *sends* the Spirit who is called the Spirit of the Son. The Father *sends* the Spirit because the Spirit proceeds from the Father; the Spirit is called the *Spirit of the Son* because the Spirit proceeds from the Son.

Sending implies the influence of one person upon the other, but the only kind of influence one divine Person has on the other is that of relationship caused by the kind of origin. All three Persons exist from all eternity; each one possesses the fullness of the divine nature; in all three there are the same divine knowledge, omnipotence, substance; all three possess the same divine intellect and will. How then do they differ?

The Father is the great "Principle or uncaused Source"; the Son is eternally begotten of the Father; the Holy Spirit proceeds from the Father and the Son as from one principle. Hence, the Son proceeds from the Father and the Holy Spirit proceeds from the Father. But if the Holy Spirit proceeded only from the Father, as does the Son, how would the Son and the Holy Spirit be distinguished from each other?

Foretelling the fact that He would send the Holy Spirit upon the apostles, our Lord says to them: "He (the Holy Spirit) will glorify me, because *he will receive of what is mine* and declare it to you. All things that the Father has are mine. That is why I have said that he will receive of what is mine, and will declare it to you" (John 16:14-15).

Perhaps the text would be clearer to English readers if we paraphrased it this way: "The Holy Spirit will fully explain or manifest Me to you, because He will be receiving then (as He always does) the fullest possession of everything that I have; and so as the Spirit of truth and illumination, He will fully show Me to you. I in turn possess always all that the Father has. That is why I speak as I do: the Father (whom you call God) communicates himself completely to Me and I communicate myself completely to the Holy Spirit. There is nothing therefore, that I can say to you that the Holy Spirit cannot make clear to you."

The Holy Spirit was not sent to the apostles simply as some kind of messenger from God declaring points of Christian doctrine. The Holy Spirit is the equal of the Father and Son in knowledge from all eternity. Proceeding as He does, from Father and Son, He possesses the full perfection of divine knowledge as well as everything belonging to the divine nature. The Father communicates the complete nature and perfection to the Son and to the Holy Spirit, but to the Holy Spirit through the Son.

This truth was perfectly clear to the Fathers of the Church from the study of Sacred Scripture in which they so gloriously excelled. But they did not always express this truth in the same language. The mystery of the Holy Trinity is so deep and impenetrable that it is difficult to find any merely human words or language that will be adequate to the task. Accordingly, two ways of speaking of the Holy Spirit's procession came into being:

1. The Holy Spirit is said to proceed "from the Father and the Son" (*ex Patre Filioque*).
2. The Holy Spirit is said to proceed "from the Father through the Son" (*ek Patròs diá Huioû*).

The first formula found favor among the Western Fathers and the second was employed by the Eastern Fathers.

St. Augustine and St. Hilary usually employed the first formula which became common in the West. In the East. St. Basil (PG 29, 656), St. Gregory Nyssa (PG 46, 1109), St. Epiphanius (PG 43, 29-32), St. Cyril of Alexandria (PG 76, 1408), employed the formula "from the Father through the Son." St. Athanasius (PG 26, 625) and St. Maximos the Confessor (PG 90, 813) do so too.

When Pope St. Martin I wrote to Constantinople that the Lateran Council (649) employed the formula "from the Father and the Son" there was much dissension and discussion among the Greek theologians. St. Maximos on this occasion eloquently defended the Latins' formula by showing that it was not really different in teaching from St. Cyril's "from the Father through the Son." In 787, St. Tarasios, who was Patriarch of Constantinople at the time, defended the correctness of both formulas at the Seventh Ecumenical Council.

Photius wrote a treatise on this doctrine denying that the Holy Spirit proceeds in any way from the Son. He used only Scriptural arguments and ignored the patristic evidence against him. His defenders say he wrote this treatise while in exile and thus was bereft of his library. But later on, in his Encyclical to the Oriental Thrones, he does invoke patristic authority by saying that both Eastern and Western Fathers favored his thesis. He cites Pope St. Leo III, for example, as being on his side simply because the Pope told Charlemagne not to allow the addition of the *Filioque* to the Creed in the Frankish dioceses. But the pope here wished merely to deny the authority of any bishop to tamper with the liturgical formulas. The pope was not denying the doctrine.

St. John Damascene has statements seeming to favor the true doctrine and then others denying that the Son be called a principle. Father Stanislaus Tyszkiewicz of Rome's Oriental Institute, points out that St. John's chief preoccupation was safeguarding the title of the Father as the sole cause in the Trinity; but the Son is joined to the Father as the one principle of the Holy Spirit. Both St. Basil and St. Gregory of Nyssa pointed out that the formula "through the Son" safeguards the title of sole cause for the Father.

Disciplinary Issue of Adding to the Creed

Both the Council of Ephesus (431) and the Council of Chalcedon (451) declared, after citing the Niceno-Constantinopolitan Creed, that no one should dare to compose another or teach any other faith. Photius, Caerularius and most of the Orthodox theologians of their time and many since, understood this injunction to refer to the literal and material form of the Creed. Western theologians contend that it means that no new doctrine may be added or any doctrine contained in it be changed. But they deny that the addition of the word "Filioque" (and the Son) adds or changes any doctrine of the Creed.

It seems that the "Filioque" was first added to the Creed by Bishop Pastor in Spain in 445, after the First Council of Toledo had approved the doctrinal point it expresses. It became common in Spain and then spread into Gaul and then eventually into Germany.

Pope St. Leo III told Charlemagne, in answer to his question about it, not to insert the word. From Pope St. Leo IX († 1054) onwards, it was generally used in the West. The Popes finally allowed the insertion, because it was doctrinally correct, but they did not command it.

At the Reunion Councils of Lyons (1274) and Florence (1438), it was agreed that as long as the East believed the correct doctrine, it was not necessary to add the "Filioque" to the Creed. It was explained that the early Councils' prohibition to add to the Creed was disciplinary only, and that really the "Filioque" did not add any new doctrine to the Creed but merely made clearer the doctrine about the procession of the Holy Spirit.

The Archpriest Sergei Bulgakov of the Paris Russian Institute concedes readily that the "Filioque" is only an explanation and not an addition to the Creed's doctrines, and other Russian Orthodox theologians concede the same point privately. Among the Greeks, however, the whole "Filioque" controversy, both as regards the doctrine and the addition to the Creed, still flourishes.

The Holy See does not require Eastern Catholics to use the "Filioque" in the Creed. The Catholic Russians and Greeks omit it; the Ukrainians and

Ruthenians generally use it.

At various times the question has been raised: Is this doctrine about the manner of the procession of the Holy Spirit really a dogma of faith or is it merely a question of varying theological opinions? The Catholic Church maintains that it is certainly a dogma of faith and defined it as such at the Reunion Council of Lyons (1274).

The general teaching of the Orthodox also maintains that the doctrine is a dogma of faith. This was strikingly brought out twice in the past hundred years.

After the First Vatican Council defined Papal infallibility, a small group of German and Dutch Catholics left the Church and founded a new sect called "Old Catholics." They made friends with the Anglicans and joined with them in an effort to unite with the Orthodox Church. For this purpose a meeting of Old Catholic, Anglican and Orthodox theologians took place at Bonn in the Rhineland in 1874-75. At these sessions the "Filioque" controversy was the great question in dispute, because the Anglicans and Old Catholics held strongly to the Catholic position. This question prevented a union.

The matter was again discussed at a Synod held in St. Petersburg, Russia, in 1892. On this occasion it was asked whether the "Filioque" doctrine was really a dogma or only a *theologoumenon* (a matter of theological opinion). A commission appointed to study the question did so for two months; they came to the conclusion that it was a dogma. This destroyed all hopes of union between the Western and Eastern non-Protestant non-Catholics.

CHAPTER 11

PURGÁTORY

Controversy regarding the existence and nature of purgatory first arose between East and West in the debates that took place in Greece in 1232 at the monastery of Kazoulos between the Franciscan Father Bartholomew and the Greek theologian Georgios Bardas. It was first listed as one of the divergencies of theology between East and West in the book published by the Dominican Fathers in Constantinople in 1252 and called *Opusculum contra Errores Graecorum.*

Purgatory was discussed at length in the Reunion Council of Florence in 1438. It was found that many of the Greeks had the Catholic doctrine confused with Origen's idea about the eventual cessation of the pains of hell. The chief anti-Western orator, Mark of Ephesus, objected strongly to the use of the term "fire," though he admitted the existence of a third or mediant state between heaven and hell. In the decree of Reunion at Florence, the Fathers carefully avoided defining "fire" as the medium of purgation.

Let us take a quick glance at the Catholic doctrine about purgatory, and the reasons for the

Church's teachings about it. Purgatory is defined as a place and state in which the souls of the just — who depart this life in a state of venial sin — suffer until all their debts have been paid. That purgatory exists and that we can help the souls detained there by prayer, especially by the holy sacrifice of the Mass, is a dogma of the Catholic faith.

There is no explicit statement about the existence and nature of purgatory to be found in Sacred Scripture. But there are several passages that very strongly suggest it, and from which we draw the logical conclusion that some place like the one we call purgatory must exist.

In the Second Book of Machabees 12:43-46, we read that Judas Machabee took up a collection of twelve thousand drachmas which he sent to the Temple in Jerusalem that sacrifices might be offered up for the soldiers who had fallen in battle, saying that "it is therefore a holy and a wholesome thought to pray for the dead, that they may be loosed from their sins."

Now even if some of the Russian theologians, under the influence of Protestant writers reject the Second Book of Machabees as a "deuterocanonical" book and not part of the genuine Scriptures, they nevertheless must admit, with Biblical scholars, that the book is a genuine record of the Machabean history. As such, then, it testifies to the traditional belief prevalent among God's people that there was such a place in the life beyond the grave, where men could atone for their sins and be released from them. This was neither heaven nor hell. We call it purgatory.

In St. Matthew's Gospel 12:32, our Lord pronounces the solemn words: "Whoever speaks against the Holy Spirit, it will not be forgiven him, either in this world or in the world to come." We are not concerned here with an analysis of the nature of the "sin against the Holy Spirit" (which is chiefly bad will blinding the intellect against God's revelation). We are concerned with our Lord's saying that there is such a thing as sin which is forgiven in the next world. Such sin is venial sin; the place of its forgiveness and atonement we call purgatory.

In the Apocalypse of St. John 21:27, we read that nothing in any way defiled can enter heaven. We also know that God wills that every man should be saved (1 Timothy 2:4). The majority of men die with at least some blemishes on their souls, for only a minority die as obvious saints. There must, therefore, be a place beyond the grave where these blemishes can be purged away so that man can enter heaven completely undefiled. This place we call purgatory.

It is hard to see how an Eastern theologian can escape the patristic evidence for purgatory in the writings of the great Greek Fathers of the Church. And yet modern booklets and articles published for Orthodox people's instruction simply content themselves with saying, "The Orthodox Church rejects the Catholic doctrine of purgatory." Such writers cannot have studied the evidence, either of Scripture or of tradition, to say nothing of a serious analysis of the meaning of their own liturgical prayers for the dead. First let us see some statements of the Greek Fathers.

St. Gregory of Nyssa († 394), in his Sermon about the Dead (PG 46, 525), says: "Man will not be able to be a partaker of divinity until a purgatorian fire will have cleansed away any stain found on his soul."

St. Cyril of Jerusalem († 386) speaks of the importance of our prayers for the dead, especially when offered up during the holy liturgy. In his immortal *Catecheses* (PG 33, 1116) we read: "If a king sent a subject into exile for his offense, and then friends of the exile came with a beautiful diadem to placate the king, wouldn't his displeasure disappear? So, too, we pray to God for the dead, not offering Him a diadem, but Christ himself slain for our sins."

St. John Chrysostom († 409) is also speaking of the power of prayer for the dead offered up at the Mass when he says (PG 62, 203): "It is not in vain that we have *received this tradition from the apostles*, that we pray for the deceased during the revered and awe-inspiring mysteries. Will not *God be appeased for them*, when all the people and priests raise their hands in supplication at this tremendous sacrifice?"

St. Maximos the Confessor († 662) has given us a work entitled *Questions and Doubts* (PG 90, 792-3) in which he answers problems that have been sent to him for solution. The 10th such question reads: "What is meant by St. Diadochos' statement that in the next life some will be judged and purged by fire?" St. Maximos answers: "Those departing this life not fully perfect must expiate that which is bad in their balance of good and bad *as if by fire.*" (The Greek says literally, "as if they were being burned" – hionéi pyroú menoi.)

In the Requiem services used by Eastern Catholics and Orthodox alike, there is repeated intercession made for the soul of the departed one, begging God to remember that He alone is the completely sinless one while all men are poor sinners.

If there is no mediant state between heaven and hell where sins may still be blotted out after death – in other words, if there be no purgatory – then what is the sense of the prayers like these litany-versicles: "Again let us pray for the repose of the soul of the departed servant of God N . . . . ,and that *every transgression*, both willful and involuntary, *be forgiven him* .... That the Lord God may establish his soul in the place where the just find rest. Let us ask for him the peace of God, the kingdom of heaven, and *the forgiveness of his sins* from Christ, our deathless King and God ... Kyrie eleison, Kyrie eleison .... "

The ordinary Russian Orthodox people must have preserved some concept of the ancient tradition of purgatory, otherwise they would not continue to refer to the time after death as the *Khozhdéniye po mukám,* the walking through torments.

CONCLUSION

Over a decade has passed since Pope John convoked Vatican Council II. The Council took place in four sessions from 1961-1964. It was brought to a successful termination by Pope Paul VI, who officially published its decrees.

Almost all the Eastern branches of Christianity not united with the Church of Rome sent delegates to the Council as "observers." These observers were tendered exquisite courtesies — such as the finest seats up front and knowledgeable priests, like the late lamented Gustave Weigel, to furnish them with running translations of the Latin speeches and functions.

Some Roman Catholic bishops, whose Latin had grown rusty over the years, were heard to remark wryly that the non-Catholics at the Council fared better than they did in knowing what was going on!

During the Council one of the most popular speakers — with repeated interventions — was the Patriarch Maximos Saigh, Melkite patriarch of Antioch. He was assisted in this Eastern apostolate by Archbishop Elias Zoghby of Egypt. These two Byzantine rite prelates ably defended Eastern views of doctrine and discipline. Orthodox observers rejoiced greatly to hear these two Eastern Catholic prelates voice what they themselves would have wished to say were they there as active participants instead of being merely passive observers.

The Council approved a decree for the Eastern Catholic Churches that is full of expressions of esteem for the Eastern liturgies and their traditions.

As a public gesture of appreciation and friendship — though not yet an act of reunion — Pope Paul for the Catholics and Patriarch Athenagoras for the Orthodox — officially annulled the excommunications that had been hurled back and forth between some Eastern and Western churchmen in the 11th century.

This is certainly in line with the eloquent words of the Orthodox Greek Bishop of Chios, the Metropolitan Panteleimon — words that appeared in the Paris daily, *Le Monde* of January 26, 1952. He says in part:

> Between the Orthodox and the Catholic Church, it is fanaticism alone that has emphasized the insignificant differences that were never serious, that existed in former times without bringing about a schism. The two most ancient churches, the Orthodox and the Catholic, should fall into one another's arms, weep over their past, and then, purified by the tears of contrition, appeal to the Divine Power and through their reconciliation, give their peoples the joy of the Lord.

In the June 1954 issue of *Ekklesia*, official organ of the Orthodox Church of Greece, an article by Professor Ioannidis of the theological faculty of the University of Athens, commemorated the ninth centenary of the calamitous separation of the East and the West. Among other things he says:

"While our differences from the Roman Catholics are very few, the links that bind us together are very many and of substantial importance. We constitute with them in fact one family because we have the same sources of faith — Holy Scripture and Holy Tradition — the same Fathers, the same saints, the same apostolic succession in the episcopal dignity, the same seven sacraments, the same holy worship, the same monastic and ascetical life, and the same understanding of the Church as the Body of Christ, as visible and invisible, although their views about the primacy have added a different emphasis to Roman Catholic opinions about the Church.

"All these are very strong motives for striving

after their cooperation and union . . . . The drawing together and collaboration and final union of the two sister churches will be brought about if we follow a policy opposite to that followed until now. Coldness and enmity widened the chasm and exaggerated the differences; love and sincerity in relations will lessen them . . . . Just as there is the Ecumenical Movement whose aim is cooperation and union of the Protestant churches among themselves and of all with the Eastern Orthodox Church, why should there not be organized also a parallel movement for cooperation and union of the two ancient churches, the Eastern and Western, which stand so very close to each other?

"Such a movement would bring Roman Catholics and Orthodox together on a spiritual plane; it would strengthen the bonds of friendship between them and would assuredly create that atmosphere of mutual respect, sympathy and love, which is essential for the promotion of the task of removing the nine-hundred-year-old schism and for the realization of the much desired and blessed union."

Much patience, good will on both sides, prayerful desire for a united Christendom, mutual charity and personal devotion to our blessed Lord who prayed for unity at the Last Supper, as well as tender love for the blessed Mother who is so loyally reverenced in both Catholic and Orthodox churches will surely produce the long-desired reunion of East and West. God wills it!

This is all in agreement with the Council's words in the decree for the Eastern Catholic churches (N. 30):

All Christians, Eastern as well as Western, are earnestly asked to pray to God fervently and insistently, indeed daily, that with the aid of the most holy Mother of God, all may become one. Let them pray also that the strength and the consolation of the Holy Spirit may descend copiously upon all those many Christians of whatever church who endure suffering and deprivations for their unwavering loyalty to the name of Christ.

'Love one another with brotherly affection; outdo one another in showing honor' (Rom. 12:10).

BIBLIOGRAPHY

Abbott, Walter. *The Documents of Vatican II.* New York, 1966.

Algermissen, Konrad. *Christian Denominations.* St. Louis, 1953.

Attwater, Donald. *The Christian Churches of the East.* 2 Vols., Milwaukee, 1948.

Dalmais-Attwater. *Eastern Liturgies.* (Twentieth Century Encyclopedia.) New York, 1960.

Dvornik, Francis. *Byzantium and the Roman Primacy.* New York, 1966.

Englert, Clement. *Eastern Catholics.* New York, 1940.
A Comparison of the Roman and Byzantine Rite. New York, 1947.
Catholics and Orthodox — Can They Unite? New York, 1961.
Christ in Christendom. New York, 1950.
The Byzantine Liturgy. New York, 1952.

Fedotov, Georgii P. *A Treasury of Russian Spirituality.* New York, 1948.

Fortescue, Adrian. *The Orthodox Eastern Church.* London, 1911.

French, Reginald M. *The Eastern Orthodox Church.* London, 1951.

Gordillo, Maurice. *Compendium Theologiae Orientalis.* 3rd ed., Rome, 1950.

Guarducci, Margherita. *The Tomb of St. Peter.* New York, 1960.

Gulovich, Stephen C. *Windows Westward.* New York, 1947.

Hanahoe, Edward and Titus Cranny. *One Fold.* Garrison, New York, 1959.

Hanssens, John. *Institutiones Liturgicae.* 2 Vols., Rome, 1930-32.

Iswolsky, Helen. *Christ in Russia.* Milwaukee, 1960.

Jacopin, Armand. *Twelfth Annual Melkite Convention.* Washington, D.C., 1971.

Janin, Raymond. *Les Eglises Orientales et les Rites Orientaux.* Paris, 1925.

Jugie, Martin. *Le Schisme Byzantin.* Paris, 1941.

> *Theologia Dogmatica Christianorum Ab Ecclesia Catholica Dissidentium.* 3 Vols., Paris, 1941.

Just, Sr. Mary. *Rome and Russia.* Westminster, Md., 1954.

King, Archdale. *The Rites of Eastern Christendom.* 2 Vols., Rome, 1947-1948.

Koncevicius, Joseph. *Russia's Attitude Towards Union With Rome.* Washington, 1927.

Kocharek, Casimir. *The Byzantine-Slav Liturgy of St. John Chrysostom.* Combermere (Ont. Can.), 1971.

LeGuillou, M. J. *The Spirit of Eastern Orthodoxy.* Vol. 135 (Twentieth Century Encyclopedia of Catholocism.) New York, 1962.

Ladomerszky, Nicholas. *Theologia Orientalis.* Rome, 1953.

Makrakis, Apostolos. *Concerning Our Duties to God.* Chicago, 1958.

Maltzew. *Die Sakramente der Orthodox-Katholischen Kirche des Morgenlandes.* Berlin, 1898.

Meyendorff, John. *The Orthodox Church.* New York, 1960.

Pospishil, Victor. *Divorce and Remarriage in the Catholic Church.* New York, 1967.

Raab, Clement. *The Twenty Ecumenical Councils of the Catholic Church.* Westminster, Md., 1959.

Raes, Alphonse. *Introductio In Liturgiam Orientalem.* Rome, 1947.

Rousseau, Olivier. "Divorce and Remarriage: East and West." *The Sacraments.* Vol. 24 of the Concilium Series. New York, 1967.

Runciman, Steven. *The Eastern Schism.* Oxford, 1955.

Sacra Congregazione Orientale. *Statistica con Cenni Storici della Gerarchia e dei Fedeli di Rito Orientale.* Rome, 1932.

Salaville, Severien. *Liturgies Orientales.* Paris, 1932.

Schmemann, Alexander. *Sacraments and Orthodoxy.* New York, 1965.

Solovyev, Vladimir. *Russia and the Universal Church.* London, 1948.

Tyciak, Julian. *Die Liturgie Als Quelle Östlicher Frömmigkeit.* Freiburg im Br., 1937.

Tyszkiewicz, Stanislaus. *Moralistes de Russia.* Rome, 1951.

Weigel, C. *El Cristianismo Oriental.* Buenos Aires, 1945.

Zvegintzov, C. *Our Mother Church.* London, 1948.